How to Be a Brilliant Teaching Assistant

.o h⌐

How to Be a Brilliant Teaching Assistant draws on knowledge from very experienced teaching assistants and Susan Bentham's own extensive research to explore the common denominators that unite all brilliant teaching assistants. The book explores becoming a brilliant teaching assistant as a journey and not an end point, and provides support that will help you along the way, whether you're just starting out in your career or you've been an experienced teaching assistant for years.

This accessible book covers all aspects of the teaching assistant role, such as:

- Key roles and responsibilities
- Meta-cognition and understanding children's learning
- Delivering high quality lessons alongside teachers
- Developing useful subject knowledge
- Undertaking research and professional development

Illustrated with activities, discussion points and anecdotes, this book is a source of support, guidance and inspiration for every teaching assistant engaged in the ongoing process of becoming an outstanding professional.

Susan Bentham is Co-ordinator of Master's Provision at the Institute of Education, University of Chichester, UK. Susan has worked at the university for ten years on a variety of programmes including Master's in Education, Master's of Teaching and Learning and the Student Associate Scheme. Her interest focuses on the training of support staff; this interest has led to the publication of nine books for teaching assistants and doctoral studies concerning collaborative relationships between teachers and teaching assistants.

How to Be a Brilliant Teaching Assistant

Susan Bentham
with Sue Sheach and Holly Saunders

Routledge
Taylor & Francis Group

LONDON AND NEW YORK

First published 2019
by Routledge
2 Park Square, Milton Park, Abingdon, Oxon OX14 4RN

and by Routledge
711 Third Avenue, New York, NY 10017

Routledge is an imprint of the Taylor & Francis Group, an informa business

British Library Cataloguing-in-Publication Data
A catalogue record for this book is available from the British Library

Library of Congress Cataloging-in-Publication Data
Names: Bentham, Susan, 1958- author.
Title: How to be a brilliant teaching assistant / Sue Bentham.
Description: Abingdon, Oxon; New York, NY: Routledge, 2019. |
Includes bibliographical references and index.
Identifiers: LCCN 2018023967 | ISBN 9781138059771 (hardback) | ISBN
9781138059788 (paperback) | ISBN 9781315163383
Subjects: LCSH: Teachers' assistants–Great Britain. | Teachers' assistants–
Training of–Great Britain.
Classification: LCC LB2844.1.A8 B44 2019 | DDC 371.14/1240941–dc23
LC record available at https://lccn.loc.gov/2018023967

ISBN: 978-1-138-05977-1
ISBN: 978-1-138-05978-8
ISBN: 978-1-315-16338-3

Typeset in Sabon
by Deanta Global Publishing Services, Chennai, India

MIX
Paper from
responsible sources
FSC
www.fsc.org   FSC® C013056

Printed and bound in Great Britain by
TJ International Ltd, Padstow, Cornwall

To the many teaching assistants, teachers and SENCos whose work has inspired this book.

Contents

Figures

Tables

Author and contributors

Dr Susan Bentham: EdD, CPsychol

Susan is currently Coordinator of Master's Provision at the Institute of Education, University of Chichester, United Kingdom. After graduating with a degree in Psychology, Susan worked for eight years in residential services for adults with learning disabilities before pursuing a career in teaching. Susan has taught Psychology in Further Education (FE), Sixth Form and Adult Education settings and taught teaching assistants on City & Guilds and NVQ courses. After achieving an MSc in Applied Psychology (learning disabilities) Susan's interest focused on the training for support staff. This interest has led to the publication of numerous books for teaching assistants. Susan has completed a Doctorate in Education and is a Chartered Psychologist.

Sue Sheach

Sue is a Senior Lecturer in Primary Education at the University of Chichester, United Kingdom, and has over thirty years of teaching experience across the primary range in mainstream, special schools and support centres and on a peripatetic learning support team. Sue has been a SENCo , Assistant Head for Inclusion and teacher in charge of a support centre for pupils with speech and language disorders. Sue is a specialist dyslexia teacher. Sue has been involved in managing and training TAs in school and at the University.

Holly Saunders

Holly has been working in the education sector for over ten years, first starting out as a TA in a school for children and young people with social, emotional and behavioural difficulties. This then led onto a career in teaching within the primary and further education sectors. Currently managing an apprenticeship department at a sixth form college, Holly has taught on the NVQ Supporting Teaching and Learning qualifications, and teaches on the Level 4 Certificate in Education and Level 5 Diploma in Education and Training. Holly has recently completed her MA in Education, where she focused on 'improving the effectiveness of TAs.'

Introduction

This book *How to Be a Brilliant Teaching Assistant* acknowledges the key role that teaching assistants play in supporting teaching and learning and has been inspired by the many teaching assistants (TAs) we have worked with over the years. Throughout this book we stress that becoming brilliant is not an end point but a continuous journey.

Though there are now many books about and for TAs on the market, we wanted this book to reflect the everyday life of a TA. Rather than simply write about what we thought was the experience of TAs, we have spent considerable time gathering the views of TAs, teachers and SENCos at the University of Chichester and Portsmouth College through questionnaires, interviews and focus groups. As such, many times in the book we will say phrases such as: 'in conducting research for this book we asked our Foundation degree students' or 'in TA interviews for our research, TAs mentioned' or 'research for the book reported that SENCos stated.' Though we recognise that the comments of those we have interviewed and surveyed will be unique to those participants we hope that by including these comments we will have communicated some of the lived experiences of teachers, SENCos and above all teaching assistants.

It is the intention that this book will be useful for TAs at varying levels of experience and with varying years of service within the classroom. Further, this book will be valuable for the teachers and SENCos who support and manage TAs. This book is written to stimulate discussion and each chapter will include: case studies, activities and discussion points. As such this book will be useful to those TAs who are enrolled on courses to include: Apprenticeships, National Vocational Qualifications (NVQs) and Foundation degrees.

This book is divided into a number of chapters to include:

Chapter 1: What's in a name? (Susan Bentham and Holly Saunders)

This chapter starts with a history of the role of the TA. Further it discusses the roles and responsibilities of a range of support staff to include: learning mentor, parent support advisor, behaviour support worker and emotional literacy support advisor. The chapter ends with a discussion on progression routes.

Chapter 2: Becoming a brilliant TA (Susan Bentham)

This chapter sets the scene for the book in that the focus is 'on becoming' and that, 'being a brilliant TA' is not an end point but an on-going journey or process. As such the importance of self-assessment, the role of reflection, learning from more experienced others, the benefits of having a mentor, the value of peer observation and on-going training will be discussed.

Chapter 3: The essentials (Susan Bentham and Sue Sheach)

The focus of this chapter is on relevant policies and guidance that TAs need to consider and reflect on in order to become a brilliant TA. These 'essentials' or key pieces of information include understanding the ethos of the school and promoting its aims and values; issues of safeguarding and confidentiality; child protection procedures; and legislation which informs practice for promoting equality, supporting pupils with special educational needs and disability and inclusive practice.

Chapter 4: Understanding learning (Susan Bentham and Sue Sheach)

Here we provide an overview of theories that explain how children learn. These theories are considered within a context of what are the optimum conditions for learning. This chapter considers the role of meta-cognition, and working memory. Further the importance of early attachment is explored.

Chapter 5: Understanding behaviour (Susan Bentham)

Appreciating that behaviour for learning is essential. This chapter will outline a pro-active style to managing the classroom environment.

Whether pupil behaviour is determined by consequences (rewards/ sanctions), feelings/emotions or thoughts, this chapter explores how an understanding of explanations can inform ways forward. As TAs work with a range of educational professionals in a variety of school contexts, attention will be paid to working effectively with others to implement school behaviour policies.

Chapter 6: Relating to others (Susan Bentham and Sue Sheach)

Here we discuss how a brilliant TA works with other people. We explore the emotional intelligence and interpersonal skills necessary to do this. A consideration of how to work with teachers, parents and other professionals is discussed, as is information about using the Local Offer to support pupils and parents.

Chapter 7: What is best practice? (Susan Bentham and Holly Saunders)

In this chapter examples of best practice evidenced from relevant research will be outlined. As such this chapter will look at implementing the advice from, *Making Best Use of Teaching Assistant Guidance Report* (Sharples et al., 2015); the recommendations from the work of Peter Blatchford and colleagues (2012, 2013) and Paula Bosanquet's and colleagues (2016) work on effective interaction.

Chapter 8: Using best practice to make a difference (Susan Bentham)

This chapter starts with a discussion on what makes for an effective intervention and the key role TAs play in interventions. Following this, the chapter goes on to present a number of case studies inspired by research and work undertaken by TAs. These case studies will focus on examples of best practice.

Chapter 9: What does a brilliant TA look like? (Susan Bentham)

This chapter will pull together all the information communicated within the book to present reflections on what it means to be brilliant. This chapter will include advice from very experienced TAs regarding what they wish someone had told them when they first started.

Chapter 1

What's in a name?

Introduction

Ever heard the phrase 'Behind every good teacher there is a great teaching assistant'? Sound about right? Well, without a doubt the support a brilliant teaching assistant (TA) could give can be endless, and if the partnership between a teacher and a TA is strong, then the result can only be an amazing educational experience for all. You see great partnerships all over the place such as, Johnny and Baby from *Dirty Dancing*, or Torvill and Dean, British ice dancers and former Olympic and World champions. When people work together and complement each other, sparks fly.

So the million dollar question is, 'How do you become a brilliant TA?' How do you make those sparks fly? How do you become the teaching assistant that is able to support pupils to reach their potential?

We hope that this book can support you on your journey to becoming brilliant or propel you towards even greater brilliance. In this chapter we aim to equip you with the necessary knowledge and understanding regarding the key roles and responsibilities of teaching assistants. But to begin this chapter focuses on the history of TAs and the key documentation related both to your role and the governance of the school. It has been said that to understand where you are going it is important first to come to terms with where you have been; as such, we explore the ever-evolving role of the teaching assistant.

But first – how many teaching assistants are there?

In reading statistical information regarding the number of TAs and teachers in schools, the numbers are often presented in terms of headcounts, that is, the actual number of individuals working in schools. However, this statistic can be misleading as the majority of teachers work full time while the majority of other staff in schools, to include TAs, work part-time. Therefore most statistical information takes account of this and presents numbers in regard to full-time equivalent (FTE) members of staff.

The 28 per cent

Let's look at the state of play in English schools from 2000 to 2013. During this time the number of TAs dramatically increased despite a slight decrease in student numbers; indeed, the number of TAs more than tripled. There were 79,000 (FTE) TAs in 2000 and 240,000 (FTE) TAs in 2013 (Masdeu Navarro, 2015, p. 10). The rise in TA numbers can be compared with the increase in teachers over this time, which was 14 per cent (Statistics UK, 2013a, 2013b). As a result, the overall student–teaching staff ratio fell dramatically.

'In November 2016 there were 957.9 thousand full-time equivalent (FTE) school workforce employees, to include classroom teachers, teachers working at leadership levels, teaching assistants, school support staff and auxiliary staff, in state-funded schools in England. 48 per cent of the schools' workforce were teachers, **28 per cent teaching assistants** and 25 per cent were non-classroom based support staff' (DfE, 2017, p. 4).

A brief history of TAs

Part 1: 1960 to 1978

As early as 1960 teaching assistants had arrived, though during this time they were referred to as general assistants or welfare assistants. As early as 1967 the Plowden Report (DES, 1967) highlighted the potential role of assistants to support teaching programmes and raise educational standards. Moyles and Sushitsky (1997), reflecting on these years, noted that welfare or general assistants were predominately women who were employed within primary schools to encourage and help pupils. Further, their responsibilities included preparing resources; collecting and returning pupils' work; first aid and undertaking lunch and break-time duties (Clayton, 1993, p. 34). In other words, these general assistants were involved in tasks such as cleaning paint pots, sharpening pencils, collecting dinner money and listening to pupils read. The year 1978 marked a pivotal point in education within this country in that the Warnock Report (DES, 1978) was published. This ground-breaking report established three key principles:

- pupils with special needs should (as far as possible) be educated in mainstream school;

- schools should promote a 'positive and challenging' approach to special educational needs (SEN) pupils that emphasised abilities and potential;
- SEN should include not only those children who attend special school but children who have transitory or continuing difficulties.

As such an increasing number of pupils with special educational needs were integrated into mainstream schools, consequentially additional staff was needed and these often were teaching assistants.

Baskind and Thompson (1995) reflecting on the Plowden (DES, 1967) and Warnock (DES, 1978) reports commented that both:

> had envisaged that assistants should be engaged because of their personal qualities, it was further expected that successful candidates would have a good general education and that continuing in-service training would be received once employed. Indeed the Plowden Report was visionary in its anticipation of future incentive allowances for additional responsibility and a planned programme of training that could provide a career route to teacher training.
>
> (p. 47)

Part 2: 1979 to 1987

The evolution and expansion of the teaching assistant continued; though, if you were working within a school at this time your official designation would probably be the 'NTA', standing for non-teaching assistant.

The 1981 Education Act (1981) was pivotal as the first piece of legislation that imposed a duty upon local educational authorities, mainstream schools and teachers to provide the necessary support to children with special educational needs so that they would be able to flourish. Again there was a further increase in the number of teaching assistants employed. Research by Hodgson, Clunies-Ross and Hegarty (1984), identified TA responsibilities during this time to include:

- Hearing children read
- Interpreting for hearing-impaired children
- Checking that pupils were 'at work'
- Preparing teaching material and other resources
- Cataloguing books
- Helping with creative activities
- Note-taking
- Engaging children in conversation

- Taking groups for home economics
- Helping children with implements during practical lessons
- Acting as an amanuensis
- Tidying the library, organizing and putting-up displays
- Helping with language programmes

(Clayton, 1993, p. 35)

During this time teaching assistants had two main roles: the first involving activities that freed 'the teacher from routine and mundane classroom activities of a non-professional nature, and the second consisting of carrying out direct instruction under the teacher's guidance' (Clayton, 1993, p. 35).

In terms of recruitment Hegarty (1985) indicated that upon starting a job as a TA, two-thirds had some professional training, usually the National Nursery Examination Board (NNEB) qualification, though most had no experience of working with pupils with SEN. In terms of conditions of work, Wigley et al. (1989) found that all TAs surveyed held temporary contracts,

> for a maximum of 27 hours per week. The number of hours can be increased or decreased at short notice. They are not paid for school holidays, but have a leave entitlement of twenty days plus statutory bank holidays.
>
> (Wigley et al., 1989, p. 3)

Part 3: 1988 to 2002

As we move from the decade that brought us the movie *ET* and the fall of the Berlin Wall into the decade that brought us the Spice Girls, *The X Files* and *Titanic*, the number of TAs within England increased again. The Education Reform Act (HMSO, 1988) introduced the national curriculum, local management of schools, a new school inspection body and stipulated national standard assessment tests to measure attainment levels; all of which added pressure to teachers. The 1989 Children's Act (1989)and 1993 Education Act (1993) further established the statutory rights of all children to receive an education appropriate to their needs and it was the school's responsibility to educate all their pupils.

In 1992 the Audit Commission acknowledged the expense of meeting the educational needs of SEN pupils. Lorenz (1992), author of books such as *Effective In-Class Support,* (1998) commented:

> Thus whether resources for children with special needs have been delegated to schools by their Local Education Authority (LEA)

or retained centrally, the need to make 'efficiencies' has become a predominant consideration. Clearly by employing assistants rather than teachers or even nursery nurses, schools and LEAs can make real savings.

(p. 27)

In 1993, the year when Michael Jordan retired from professional basketball, Terrance Clayton, commented that:

> The role of the British classroom assistant has developed over the last quarter of a century from one of care and housekeeping to now include substantial involvement in the learning process itself. Today's classroom assistants, particularly those working in mainstream schools with children with special educational needs, could well be described as 'assistant teachers'. However, one should add in caution that they serve in a supportive capacity under the day-to-day supervision of the class teacher whose role also seems to be changing towards that of 'classroom manager'.
>
> (Clayton, 1993, p. 42)

The next landmark event was the publication of the first Code of Practice on Identification and Assessment of Children with Special Educational Needs (DfE, 1994). This document recognised the legal entitlement of students, designated as having a 'statement' to additional provision and support, which set about once again a dramatic increase in the numbers of TAs employed within schools.

Though the Warnock Report had outlined the aim of inclusion in 1978, more pupils with special needs integrated into mainstream schools in response to the 1996 Education Act necessitated greater pupil support. By 1999 The Centre for Studies of Inclusive Education (CSIE) proclaimed that there were no legitimate reasons to separate children within special schools for the duration of their schooling.

Of course, all these changes to include the introduction of the national curriculum and the increasing number of children identified with SEN within mainstream schools added greatly to the teachers' workload. To some extent the pressure on teachers was offset by additional responsibilities given to TAs, though there were criticisms that the most vulnerable and needy pupils were being supported by staff with the least qualifications.

An editorial in the magazine *Special Children* April 2001 writes:

> Mrs Overall to the fore …
>
> If you were the parent of a child with special needs, which type of support would you prefer for him? A teacher, or a cleaning lady? You may well be thinking 'no competition' but pause for a moment and re-consider this from a headteacher's point of view. Your budget is stretched. You have to be seen to be 'doing something' about providing for pupils with special needs you can't afford to employ a teacher – even if you could find one. Mrs Overall is a very pleasant lady. She has attended four days training as a classroom assistant and she is cheap. She also happens to be one of the school's cleaning ladies. Far-fetched? Not at all. This is a true reflection of the situation in many schools at the moment.
>
> (p. 3)

A further article written in *The Evening Standard* (Gilman, 2001) tells the story of one teaching assistant:

> Here was my chance to make a difference. Early last year; I heard about a vacancy at a local school that sounded ideal. Keen to help students achieve their potential, as I had failed to do, I jumped at the opportunity. I assumed I would get some training. Surely they wouldn't take somebody off the street and chuck them straight into a classroom with the most disruptive students? But that's exactly what they did. My fellow teaching assistants advised me to make it up as I went along.
>
> (p. 28)

To counter these criticisms of lack of training, programmes to include NVQs based on National Occupational Standards (LGNTO, 2001), were introduced. Further, in 2001 Foundation Degrees for Teaching Assistants were introduced in England (Dunne et al., 2008). These Foundation degrees were designed as a flexible higher education '*vocation focused qualification*', which aimed to integrate academic and work-based learning.

In 2001 the labour government released the Special Educational Needs (SEN): Code of Practice (DfEE, 2001), which outlined a staged approach to meeting the needs of pupils with SEN to include: early identification, school action, school action plus and statements of special educational needs, with provision often expressed in numbers of hours of TA support.

In 2001, the PriceWaterhouseCoopers Teacher Workload Study Final Report responded to concerns regarding teacher workload and proposed solutions, which in part advocated supporting teachers and reducing workload through the effective and efficient use of staff other than teachers. This was supported and recognised by an HMI report (Ofsted, 2002), which suggested that the quality of teaching in lessons where TAs were present is better than in lessons without them.

Part 4: 2003 to 2008

In the year 2003 when England won the Rugby World Cup with Jonny Wilkinson's famous drop goal, the Department for Education and Skills published the Raising Standards and Tackling Workload: a national agreement (DfES, 2003). This document became known as the Remodelling Agenda or Agreement. The Agreement promised teachers that ten per cent of their teaching time would be set aside for Planning, Preparation and Assessment (PPA) beginning 2005 and that coverage for this time need no longer be provided by qualified teachers. The Agreement set out the role of the Higher Level Teaching Assistant (HLTA) who would be able to cover PPA time. Crucially, the agreement paved the way for individuals without Qualified Teacher Status (QTS) to undertake activities previously confined to only qualified teachers. The impact of the changes advocated by the Agreement were said to strike at the heart of teacher professionalism. Research into the deployment and impact of support staff who achieved HLTA status (Wilson et al., 2007, p. 9) proclaimed that it was 'clear that the HLTA role has the potential to change the way in which education is delivered and to make a positive difference to school life.' However, it was noted that the practice of split contracts for support staff was widespread; that is, a teaching assistant, including those who meet the higher level HLTA standards, will only receive enhanced pay for those hours when they are specifically deployed in an HLTA capacity (WAMG, 2008).

Howes (2003, p. 147), in reviewing the literature on the impact of teaching assistants, concluded that further research and attention needed to be given to the role of paid adult support in respect to:

- The role TAs had in regard to not only of raising standards but also their role in contributing to pupils' 'engagement in learning';
- The risk of TAs inadvertently marginalising pupils through isolated support;
- The important mediating role that TAs can play between school, teachers and children or young people.

Referring back to the article written in the *Evening Standard* (Gillman, 2001) the author reflects:

> One pupil I was supporting was in a high-ability set but had mild dyslexia which meant he could be slow to copy things down. I decided that the best strategy was to sit with him and make sure he was keeping up. All seemed well for a couple of weeks but then I bumped into a teacher who was responsible for this student's special needs input (I had not been informed of her existence). I explained I had been sitting next to our student and helping him. She looked aghast and told me that this was inappropriate as it could draw attention to the student and make him even more self-conscious and withdrawn. Instead, I should make a point of circulating round the class, helping anyone who needed it but keeping a discreet eye on our pupil.
>
> (p. 28)

Lorenz (2002) in writing guidance for TAs outlined three types of support:

- The TA that is Velcro-ed to the pupils they support. This way of working does not allow the pupil to relate to others in their class and may make pupils feel even more isolated;
- the TA who is compared to the hovering helicopter, always at hand if anything goes wrong and;
- the ideal type, 'the bridge builder' who creates with the teacher learning opportunities that the pupil can do and opportunities where the pupil can interact in a positive manner with other pupils.

In 2004 the labour government published the *Every Child Matters* document (DfES, 2004), which set out to provide a framework for services that aimed to both protect children and young people and maximise their potential. The document promoted five outcomes:

Being healthy
Staying safe
Enjoying and achieving
Making a positive contribution and
Economic well-being

The aim of this document was to reduce the numbers of children who experienced educational failure, engaged in offending or anti-social behaviour, suffered from ill health or became teenage parents. In a review of the impact of the Every Child Matters (ECM) Agenda (Lewis et al., 2007) it was noted that though schools, to include teaching staff, had made good progress in implementing the agenda, the main challenge for schools was to develop closer collaborative working relationships with other services involved in supporting children and young people.

Though the impact of TAs had been researched over the last decades it was in 2003 when Peter Blatchford and colleagues at the University College London's Institute of Education conducted one of the largest studies of its type. The study, the Deployment and Impact of Support Staff (DISS) ran for six years and:

> sought to provide a rigorous description of the characteristics and deployment of support staff, including the nature of their activities and interactions with pupils, and to address their impact on teachers, teaching and pupils.
>
> (Blatchford et al., 2012, p. 8)

Part 5: 2009 to 2013

In 2009 Peter Blatchford and colleagues finished their six-year Deployment and Impact of Support Staff (DISS project). Results from the project concluded that while TAs had a positive effect on teachers in terms of workload, job satisfaction and stress, it was found that the more a TA supported a pupil the less progress they made (Blatchford et al., 2012).

These findings, both beneficial in terms of teacher satisfaction and troubling in regard to negative outcomes on pupil progress, were explained by the authors using the Wider Pedagogical Role (WPR) model (Blatchford et al., 2012). This model provided a detailed picture of factors impacting the quality of support staff work and acknowledged that the negative effects of TAs could be attributed to aspects of preparedness and deployment, that is, aspects outside the control of support staff (for further details see Chapter 7).

Following on from the DISS report (Blatchford et al., 2012) the Effective Deployment of TAs (EDTA) (Blatchford et al., 2013) project took place between 2010 and 2011. The project used as a starting point the implications of the Wider Pedagogical Role (WPR) model to explore alternative strategies in order to empower schools to release the untapped potential of their TAs. The aim of the EDTA study was to work in collaboration with headteachers, teachers and TAs in order to develop school-based strategies for effective TA deployment and practice in mainstream schools. Effective strategies included: creating liaison time between teachers and TAs; ensuring that TAs worked more often with middle- and high-attaining pupils while teachers worked with low attaining and SEN pupils. They also encouraged TAs to ensure interactions with pupils were focused on understanding rather than task completion (Blatchford et al., 2013).

Part 6: 2013 and beyond

After 14 years of the SEN Code of Practice (DfEE, 2001), the code was redeveloped and the Special Educational Needs and Disability Code of Practice: 0 to 25 years (DfE, DoH, 2015) emerged. The code of practice was statutory guidance for organisations working with children and young people that had a special educational need or disability. The important points from the Code of Practice included: a clearer focus on the views of children and young people and parents in decision making; an emphasis on close co-operation between education, health services and social care and importantly that:

> teachers are responsible and accountable for the progress and development of the pupils in their class, even where pupils access support from teaching assistants or specialist staff.
>
> (Paragraph 6.36, p. 99)

In 2014 The Education Endowment Foundation (EEF) Teaching and Learning Toolkit, was published and presented as a research-based guide that compared the impact of initiatives and resources on pupils' attainment with their cost. Following on from this, the Education Endowment Foundation released the 'Making Best Use of Teaching Assistant Guidance Report' (Sharples et al., 2015), for schools, which outlined recommendations to maximise the impact of teaching assistants. More on this will be presented in Chapter 7.

Perhaps as a final comment to our discussion on the history of TAs, it is important to return to pay and conditions. A recent *Times Education Supplement* article (2017) outlined a number of contract options available to TAs including:

- Permanent all year
- Temporary all year
- Permanent term time
- Temporary term time
- Casual

In regard to contracts amongst local authorities, the vast majority of TAs are on term-time or casual contracts with TAs are most likely to be on a limited pay scale ranging from around £13,600 to a maximum of around £15,900 per annum (*TES*, 2017). However, in commenting on pay and conditions, *the Guardian*'s Secret Teaching Assistant (*The Guardian*, 2016) reflects:

> I originally planned to have career in teaching, but I soon realised the benefits of working as a teaching assistant (TA). Granted, the pay leaves a lot to be desired, but we are privileged to be able to develop close, supportive relationships with the pupils who need it most.

Discussion point

A pause to reflect

If we take a moment and look at the past 60 years of TA deployment it is safe to say a lot has happened to both the TA role and the educational system they work within.

Within the historical review, a number of recurring themes have emerged to include:

Changing roles and responsibilities;
Pay and conditions;
The need for training;
The professional relationship between TA and teacher;
The impact of inclusion;
The impact of government policies on schools.

Further, various terms have been used to describe the role of the TA over the years to include:

Welfare assistant
Jill of All trades? (Moyles and Sushitsky, 1997)
An Extra Pair of Hands? (Wilson et al., 2003)
Mum's Army

But, what can we learn from the evolving history of TAs? From your view, working in schools now:

What has changed over the years?
What has remained the same?
What in your opinion is the way forward?

Activity 1.1 A day in the life

From the case study below can you guess the year? On what basis have you made you decision?

It's a Monday morning and Mrs Price, the TA, arrives at the school early (7:45a.m.) even though she is not officially paid until (8:45a.m.), as she values the time she has with the class teacher to set up and talk about the day ahead. It is just after break and Mrs Watson, the class teacher, is trying to get the class ready for English. Mrs Watson calls out: 'Children come on, tidy your math books away, where did you get that football David? It's nearly time for English!' Some children listened, and started to put their books away, others still distracted kept on playing. Mrs Watson continued, 'David please put away that football! Stanley don't push Charlie over!' Mrs Price, the TA, has started to read out children's names, 'Alan, David, Linda, come with me it's time to read.' Mrs Watson shouts above the ever-increasing noise, 'Year 2! Please come and sit on the carpet! Mrs Price after you have heard Alan, David and Linda read, can you prepare the resources for art this afternoon?' 'Of course!' Mrs Price, the TA, replied. 'Thank you! I wouldn't know what I would do without you!' exclaims Mrs Watson.

Roles and responsibilities

So back to the title of this chapter, 'what's in a name?' Often the first piece of information we have about someone is their name and what they do, and we use this information to form impressions. So it seems there is a lot to a name!

From our brief history lessons, we have a better understanding of how the roles of teaching assistants have evolved over time. Not only have their roles and responsibilities changed, but also their titles. TAs can have many different interchangeable and overlapping roles and responsibilities throughout the day, all equally important.

Getting to grips with the many different TA roles can be like learning a new language. A lack of understanding this language can make you feel, at first, like an outsider; so let's now look at these diverse roles outlined in Table 1.1.

Table 1.1 Roles and responsibilities

Role	Aims	Responsibilities
TA or Classroom Assistant	To support the teacher and pupil's learning.	Preparing the classroom Creating and preparing resources Supporting pupil(s) with their learning Supporting with behaviour management Pastoral care of pupils Carrying out interventions under guidance Supporting with general classroom management
Learning Support Assistant (LSA)	To work with the teacher to prepare and deliver learning programmes and support to individual pupils, or groups.	TAs and LSAs are often thought to have similar roles. While these terms are often used interchangeably the definitions of these roles will vary between schools. However, learning support assistants usually have a more pastoral role and will often be hired to undertake intervention programmes. Responsibilities include: • supporting pupils with specific needs whether special education needs or gifted and talented learners on a 1:1 basis, or as a group; • may often be tasked to support certain pupils; • carrying out interventions, as directed by the teacher which tend to be outside the classroom, and; • liaise with the special educational needs co-ordinator (SENCo) regarding pupils they have been assigned to support.
Learning Mentor	The aim of a learning mentor is to support pupils and in doing so will collaborate with teachers, senior managers, parents, care givers and other agencies thus helping to create a network of support.	Learning mentors provide support and guidance to help pupils who are experiencing difficulties in learning due to social, emotional or behavioural problems. Learning mentors can work with children and young people of all ages and can work with pupils individually or in small groups. Responsibilities include: • working with other relevant educational professionals to select pupils for mentoring; • discussing the aims of mentoring with pupils; • agreeing and writing action plans to support underperforming pupils both inside and outside of the classroom.

Role	Description	Details
Parent Support Advisor	To work with schools, pupils and families to resolve concerns around low attendance and helps parents to support their children's learning.	May identify concerns or problems and offer advice or solutions to support attendance. Parent Support Advisors will facilitate the building of relationships between parents and schools. They may also help to arrange alternative education for pupils who are excluded and may make referrals on to other agencies.
Behaviour Support Worker/Advisor	To provide specialist advice and support for individuals with challenging behaviour.	May include carrying out behavioural assessments and producing recommendations, implementing behavioural interventions, and liaising with external agencies as appropriate. Behaviour support workers/advisors may also deliver training to staff teams in how to deal with challenging behaviour.
Emotional Literacy Support Assistant (ELSA)	To support the emotional needs of pupils.	There is both a national recognition and concern regarding the rising number of young people with mental health needs. Schools have an important role to play in supporting pupils with a range of emotional difficulties, from those who appear withdrawn to those who have challenging behaviour. The Emotional Literacy Support Assistant, with appropriate training and support, can enhance pupils' emotional literacy, behaviour, self-esteem, emotional wellbeing, peer relationships and resilience.
Higher Level Teaching Assistant (HLTA)	To support the teaching and learning with a greater level of responsibility.	The Higher Level Teaching Assistant (HLTA) role was introduced in 2003. This role is awarded to TAs who meet the national HLTA standards. An HLTA does all the things that regular TAs do, with the key difference being the increased level of responsibility. HLTAs will have additional responsibilities to include: teaching classes and covering planned absences.
Apprentice TA	To train as a TA while learning at college and gaining a qualification.	Apprentice TAs will have similar responsibilities to teaching assistants, though there is an understanding that they will be studying for qualifications or meeting standards as part of their apprenticeship. Apprentice TAs are to be treated the same as any other member of staff with the understanding that they are learning, and so have certain limitations in regards to responsibilities and to what they can achieve.

TA responsibilities will vary from school to school; however, whether they have a pedagogical focus (on the learning) or a non-pedagogical focus (pastoral role) their ultimate aim, whether direct or indirect, is to support learning and teaching and ultimately aid pupils to achieve their potential.

For those readers wanting to become a TA our next activity may help, and it may be of interest for those already in post who have responsibilities for supporting new TAs. When applying for a TA role it is worth noting that jobs in education mainly appear at certain points of the year. These are normally at the beginning of school term, with the job market really opening up from May to July. This is when people normally look to move to another school.

Teaching assistant job description at Everyday Primary

Job purpose

- To enable pupils to access learning by supervising and assisting pupils across a wide range of activities and supported learning activities.
- To promote the development of the physical and mental wellbeing of pupils as directed by a teacher.
- Contribute to the effective organisation of the school with administrative and clerical support.

Key accountabilities

- To actively promote and comply with the School's Policies and Procedures relating to: safeguarding, health and safety, equal opportunities, and data protection.
- To work closely with colleagues to achieve and plan objectives and targets.
- To participate in employee development schemes and performance management, and contribute to the identification of own team development needs.

Principle responsibilities/duties

Curriculum support

- Assist with the planning of learning activities by identifying and preparing resources required to support lesson plans and learning outcomes.
- Preparation of materials/equipment (e.g. books, pencils, art supplies, games, IT equipment) and clearing up activities with the pupils.
- Maintaining classroom resources and designated areas.
- Supervise individuals or small groups of pupils undertaking teacher-led learning activities by coordinating and explaining basic instructions for the activity, adjusting activities within the scope of the lesson plan in response to pupils' learning needs.
- Assisting pupil achievement by monitoring learning against learning outcomes and informing the teacher of progress.
- Assist pupils to develop their independence.
- Support the use of IT as a tool to enable learning.
- Arrange the classroom to create a positive learning environment including classroom displays.
- Assist in the supervision of children in the playground, supporting the teacher in ensuring the maintenance of high standards of behaviour. Work on play skills with individual children.
- Assist at lunch time either in the hall helping and encouraging children to learn the social skills of mealtimes, or in the playground encouraging co-operative interaction.

General school support

- Be involved in extra-curricular activities (e.g. clubs, activities, trips, open days, presentation evenings).
- Within the working day be available to support teaching staff through the production of teaching resources.
- Report student and school issues in line with the school's policies for health and safety, child protection, safeguarding and behaviour management, etc.

- Attend all staff meetings and professional development sessions as required.
- Any additional responsibilities as directed by your line manager.

Discussion point

Thinking about your role

What are the key TA responsibilities that the school requires from this TA?
How does this job description differ from your own role as a TA?
How could an experienced TA support another TA who is just starting out in meeting these responsibilities?

Progression routes

Once in post there are a number of progression routes open to TAs. Progression can be achieved through the gaining of additional qualifications, and/or through completing professional development relevant to your role; both will increase your experiences and enhance your practice. Outlined in Table 1.2 are a range of qualifications, starting with Level 1 and concluding with teacher training and postgraduate opportunities. Please note that the specific titles of awards and qualifications may vary between training providers, colleges and universities.

When considering your future it is important that you gain impartial and appropriate advice, some of the following points may be worth considering:

- **Online courses:** Research the credentials of online courses as some may not be attached to any recognised qualification or credit transfer system;
- **Do your research:** Speak to colleagues or career advisors within local colleges or universities. If the opportunity arises attend open days;
- **Consider your options:** What do you want to achieve? How long will it take you? How much will it cost?

As outlined in Table 1.2 there are numerous progression opportunities, but it is always helpful to hear the career journeys other TAs have taken. The following case studies will reflect a range of progression routes that TAs can follow within the education sector.

Table 1.2 Progression routes

Level	Qualifications	Description
1	Entry level qualifications for post-16 courses	Level 1 courses include BTEC diplomas and NVQ 1 and GCSE's grades (D-G)
2	National Vocational Qualification (NVQ) Certificate in Supporting Teaching and Learning in Schools Teaching Assistant Apprenticeship	NVQ qualifications develop a TAs practical skills and knowledge and cover areas such as: safeguarding, learning strategies, communication, and understanding the school context. Typical individuals undertaking these qualifications will either be employed in a school or working within a school as a volunteer.
3 (equivalent to A levels)	National Vocational Qualification (NVQ) Diploma in Specialist Support for Teaching and Learning in Schools Teaching Assistant Apprenticeship	This apprenticeship programme has a set of standards that an apprentice must meet, which can include a qualification. The aim of this standard is to give schools more autonomy over their apprentices learning programme. Apprentices need to be working within a school or education setting in order to complete the programme.
4 (Higher education courses at early degree level)	Higher Level Teaching Assistant	A set of professional standards that an experienced TA must demonstrate. These include: Professional Values and Practice, Knowledge and Understanding, and Teaching and Learning activities. The HLTA designation is a 'status' and not a qualification.
	Foundation Degree in Teaching and Learning Support	Designed to further your knowledge and understanding of how to support teaching and learning of pupils. Often foundation degrees are designed so that if you wish to gain a full degree, there are opportunities to do so. Foundation degrees are level 4 in the first year and level 5 in the second.
	Certificate in Education	This qualification, at Level 4, for the post-16 (further education/lifelong learning) sector aims to develop an understanding and knowledge of the roles and responsibilities of a teacher/trainer, and the necessary skills in delivering and assessing in education and training. This qualification will enable progression on the Level 5 Diploma in Education and Training.

5	Diploma in Education and Training	The Level 5 Diploma in Education and Training are recognised teaching qualifications for the post-16 (further education/lifelong learning) sector. After completion of Level 5 individuals wishing to extend their qualifications for teaching in the post-16 sector (further education/ lifelong learning) can apply for the Professional Graduate Certificate of Education and Training, Level 6.
6	BA (Hons) Education Studies	A three year degree (Level 4-6) designed to develop your knowledge and understanding of education, and includes the opportunity to carry out research. Individuals successfully completing this degree may choose to progress to train as a teacher.
		The Qualified Teacher Learning and Skills (QTLS) is a designation awarded to teachers in the Further Education (FE) sector.
7 (post-graduate level)	Teacher Training – PGCE or Schools Direct (QTS)	These programmes require a degree and would be a route for individuals wishing to become qualified primary school or secondary school teachers.

Case study 1.1: From TA to teacher to aspiring special educational needs co-ordinator (SENCo)

Shaun worked at a maintained secondary school as a TA and then as a cover supervisor before moving to work in the Further Education (FE) sector. Shaun's line manager commented that he had a real aptitude for teaching and as such, Shaun enrolled for and completed the Level 4 Certificate in Education, and then the Level 5 Diploma in Education and Training. Indeed, his college paid for Shaun to attend this training as part of his professional development. Shaun then applied for the Qualified Teacher Learning and Skills (QTLS) Level 6. Shaun is now a qualified teacher working in an FE college supporting students with SEN.

Case study 1.2: From apprentice TA to degree

At the age of 17 Mable knew she had a passion for working with children. Mable completed her Level 2 Teaching Apprenticeship and then progressed to the Level 3 Teaching Assistant Apprenticeship while at the same time completing her Level 4 Certificate in Education. Mable has now enrolled to do the Foundation Degree at a local university and aspires to be a teacher.

Case study 1.3: From TA to HLTA to art therapist

Danielle has worked as a TA going on 17 years. In 2003 she gained her NVQ 3 and two years after she gained the HLTA status. Danielle's line manager has always encouraged her to consider a role in teaching, but Danielle has always been very busy with her four children. But now that the youngest has left for university Danielle feels it is 'me time' and she would like to follow her dream to become an art therapist. Danielle believes that art therapy will help her with her role in the behaviour support unit. Danielle did think of becoming a teacher, but actually she loves being a TA and an HLTA.

Discussion point

What is your dream?

Considering these case studies, which one appeals to you?

Can you see that there are many routes, not just the conventional ones?

Each case study describes someone who has followed their dream. What is your dream?

Summary

So as in true educational style we are doing a 'plenary'. Hopefully you've gained a better understanding of the history of TAs, the main roles a TA has, training opportunities for TAs and progression opportunities available to them. Before moving on to the next chapters we would like to introduce you to two influential writers.

- Build a good relationship with the teacher; this can be difficult at times because of work and time pressures, but it is worthwhile and very beneficial. Be clear about what the teacher's expectations are. Be organised, proactive and responsive. Remember you are the teacher's eyes and ears in the classroom!
- Work closely with the teacher. Develop good classroom management strategies. Get to know class routines. Be aware of the lessons plans. Think ahead regarding resources that are needed. Get to know your pupils well. Ensure support is available to the pupil when necessary but ensure that this support doesn't prevent pupil independence;
- Practice, read lots and ask lots of questions;
- Observe good practice and adapt your own working practice to match this. Remember you will continue to learn new strategies for dealing with situations as no one situation is the same;
- Be willing to help in any way you can and be prepared for any challenges you may face. Realise that no matter how long you are a TA there will always be challenges;
- Take on-board advice and criticism;
- Start with a passion for wanting to help children and wanting to improve their outcomes.

Knowing and knowledge

TAs who answered our questionnaire regarding, 'what qualities make for a brilliant TA' came up with an amazing list of responses and certainly one common theme within their replies was the role of learning. So perhaps in the pursuit of understanding how to become brilliant it is helpful to start with a discussion on learning, that is, the role of knowing and the means of gaining knowledge.

First we can say that we have knowledge of ourselves, our strengths, what we already know and the areas we need to develop. We can call this aspect of knowing – self-awareness. I can remember my first line manager saying that the art of knowing how to do your job well is to both know who to ask for help and when to ask. And of course our knowledge in relation to our job would include knowing relevant school policies, specific theories regarding how pupils learn and knowing how to relate to others.

One useful way of thinking about knowing is illustrated by the views of who sees knowledge as the foundation for action but argues that more than just knowledge is needed to become an effective practitioner or a brilliant TA. Here we are reminded of the expression that not only do we need to 'talk the talk' but we need to 'walk the walk'. Perhaps it is helpful to compare the knowledge involved in teaching and facilitating pupil learning to the skills needed to drive a car. Most of us in learning to drive would have passed a theory test long before we mastered the art of driving and could successfully negotiate a busy roundabout or parallel park!

Miller (1990) in writing about assessment in education focused *not on what was taught* but *on what was learnt* and more importantly what learners could do with the knowledge as demonstrated through action. Miller's (1990, p. S63) model of assessment is portrayed as a pyramid with 4 levels to include:

1 *Lowest level*: Knows (knowledge)
2 Knows how (competence)
3 Shows how (performance)
4 *Highest level*: Does (Action)

Activity 2.1 Can you apply Miller's model to aspects of your job? (One example is given)

Example	Knowledge	Knows how	Shows how	Does (action)
What do I know about giving effective praise?	I know that praise focusing on effort encourages a growth mindset.	I know that if a child says that they can't do maths – I should say, 'You mean, you can't do this yet!'	In an observation my teacher observed me saying, 'You mean, you can't do this yet!' to a pupil and praised me for saying this. The teacher then said I could have discussed with the pupils what strategies they could use. The teacher also reminded me to praise effort, *but only if effort is connected with actual learning.*	I need to remember to do *all of this in all my conversations* with pupils.
What do I know about what makes an effective question?				
What do I know about enabling pupils to be independent learners?				

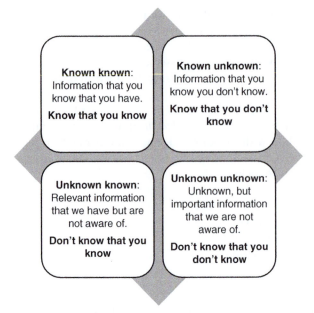

Figure 2.1 Types of knowns and unknowns.

Figure 2.1 *Types of Knowns and Unknowns* outlines various types of knowing. Though at first glance this seems incredibly confusing, it is a very useful reflection point for considering what we do and do not know and what we need to know to become a brilliant TA.

Consider the category: Known unknown – Knowing that you don't know

There is a well-known adage that goes, 'The more you know, the more you realise how much you don't know – the less you know, the more you think you know'.

Theorists would argue that this knowing what you don't know is what underpins curiosity and drives us to discover more. Though theories of learning will be discussed in greater depth in Chapter 4, Piaget believed that the uncomfortable feeling that you get *when you know that you don't know*, what he described as **cognitive disequilibrium**, is the motivation to learn!

Consider the category: Unknown known – Don't know what you know

This aspect of not knowing that you know relates to what is referred to as tacit knowledge (Schön, 1983). Everyone has a vast reservoir of tacit knowledge; that is, we know more than we can often communicate or say. This unwritten, unspoken, unconscious knowledge is often based on emotions, experiences, insights and intuition.

Imagine the following situation:

The Headteacher asks a new TA to sit in and observe a very experienced TA's practice. The new TA observes the experienced TA working with her group and notes how well she gets on with all the pupils in her group, how she seems to know exactly what to say to encourage and inspire them. At the end of the session the conversation goes as follows:

New TA: That was an amazing session. You got on so well with all of the pupils and I know that some of them are tricky. How did you do it? What is your secret?

Experienced TA: Actually I don't know how I do it ... I have done this for so long – it is just me.

In this example the experienced TA has what is referred to as tacit knowledge. However, the limitations of tacit knowledge are that the experienced TA is not able to articulate or share her good practice with others. In order to move forward the experienced TA needs to think hard about how she does what she does in order to make her knowledge explicit to both herself and then to others.

The Headteacher discussing this with the experienced TA states:

> There is a tendency to identify our successes with the successful things we have done. If the pupils have done well then we have done a great job! However, in order to be truly brilliant you need to be able to share your good practice with others. In order to develop your own practice you need to *reflect* not only on what the pupils were doing but to *reflect* on what *you were doing* to enable them to do well. It is not enough to say 'I don't know how I do it'.

To become brilliant you need to know how you make a difference!

Activity 2.2 Reflecting on types of knowns and unknowns

Try to give an example for each of the categories below. For some of these categories you may need to talk to relevant colleagues. To help you get started examples have been provided:

	Example	Your example
I know that I know	I know that I know theories of what makes praise effective. We discussed this at our last INSET day.	
I know that I don't know	I have heard many people talk about growth mindsets. I know that I know a little about this but I know there is much that I don't know.	
I don't know that I know	My teacher says I have mastered the art of questioning. To tell you the truth I was surprised by this as I do not know any theory about questioning techniques – I just talk.	
I don't know that I don't know.	The HLTA said to me that our school needs to look into scaffolding. I immediately thought they were referring to the fact that we needed to get the school windows painted and perhaps we needed to get some quotes from scaffolding companies. My brother has his own scaffolding company. I mentioned this to the Headteacher and she said that this is not what the HLTA was talking about. Now that I know this… it is not the case that I *don't know that I don't know*… but that I **know** that I don't know!	

Reflection

Reflection is a word that has many meanings. When asked to define reflection one person may comment about noting her reflection in a mirror, for example, 'I was shopping and caught a glance of myself in a mirror and was horrified by what I was wearing – why on earth did I think that coat made me look slim'. In terms of the field of education and professional practice, reflection begins with the concept of self-awareness, that is, in a sense holding a mirror up to yourself and your actions.

As professionals engaged in teaching we can both reflect in the moment and after the event. Have you ever been involved in a teaching session and realise that it is just not going as you would like it to? Perhaps in the moment of teaching you are suddenly aware that despite your careful planning and considered questioning the pupils do not seem to understand what you are trying to explain to them. Maybe at that moment you are consciously aware that in order for the pupils to learn you need to change your approach and so you do. This is what Schön (1983) refers to as reflection in action.

On the other hand, more likely at the end of the day, driving home, or as you are cooking dinner, your mind may wander back to a particular event that went very well or perhaps did not go as you would have hoped. Perhaps you wake up in the middle of the night and think about things you should have said or things you should have done and things you must remember to do tomorrow. This is what Schön (1983) refers to as reflection on action.

To be brilliant TAs need to do both, that is, reflect on action and reflect in action.

In order for reflection to be used to its potential as a constructive means for improving practice, reflection needs to be considered. As such many models of reflection have been developed.

A model of reflection

There are many models of reflection but a useful one for recording and making sense of experiences (Reflection on action) has been developed by Gibbs (1988). Gibbs talks of a reflective cycle which involves:

Description of the event: This section requires a brief description of what happened or what should have happened.

Feelings: This requires you to describe both your feelings and thoughts. Remember there is a link between how you think and how you feel. It is also helpful to record how you think others felt and on what basis do you know this. It might also be important to reflect on how confident you felt in the situation.

Evaluation: This is the part where we make a professional judgement in regards to our performance and the extent to which we enabled the pupils to meet their learning objectives. Remember evaluation does not always have to be negative; it is equally important to record and reflect on our successes.

Analysis: Here we are trying to make sense of what happened. What factors or educational theories can be used to explain what happened? Again it is important to bring this analysis to our successes as well as those incidents that did not go as well as we had hoped. As we have stated previously, in terms of our successes, when a new colleague asks us to explain the secret to a great session it is not enough, nor very helpful for the new colleague, for us to respond with a comment such as, 'I know it was a great session, but actually I really don't know how I do it – it is just the way I am'.

In conclusion: This is a summary statement regarding what other actions you could have taken.

Action plan: This involves outlining your next steps in regard to your professional journey. If the situation were to occur again what would you do?

Case study 2.1: Working with the Nightingale group

Sadie was a TA in a large primary school and working in a Year 2 classroom. Sadie was assigned to work with the Nightingale group. The teacher had requested the pupils to write a letter, from the perspective of an archaeologist searching for treasures in Egypt, to their family in England. Sadie reflects:

Description of the event

There were five children in the Nightingale group and all of them needed encouragement and help with the spelling and sentence construction. I decided to go round the group first and ask each of them what they were going to include in their letters home. I asked James first, and he said he was going to talk about how hot it was and how he didn't like the food. Charlie said he was going to talk about digging. Danny said he was going to talk about monster spiders. The boys seemed very enthusiastic and then it was Daisy's turn and she said, 'I don't know what to write'. I said, 'Well the boys have come up with some really good ideas and perhaps you could also talk about the sand and the heat and the spiders'. James then said, 'No she can't those are our ideas!' Daisy got more upset and said, 'I don't like your silly ideas anyway'. Daisy then put her head down on the desk. I told James that we share our ideas and then I said to Daisy, 'Well you just have a think, sometimes closing your eyes and putting your head on the desk helps you think'. Then Adele, Daisy's friend, put her head on the desk and said she also wanted to think. I left Daisy and Adele to think and went over to the boys to look at their work. At this point the teacher came over and asked Daisy and Adele what they were doing. Daisy and Adele started to giggle and said they were thinking. The teacher commented that they could think just as well sitting up properly. After the teacher left I told Daisy and Adele that if they didn't start writing that they would have to stay in at break time.

Feelings	I felt that I didn't handle the situation as well as I could have. I should have been able to motivate Daisy and Adele to work. Perhaps I should have been firmer with James.
Evaluation	The boys produced some very good work, however the girls only managed to write one sentence each.
Analysis	I think that the boys were already very interested in the idea of explorers so this was an easy task for them. I feel that the girls just didn't have the same interest. Daisy and Adele are 'very girly' girls.
In conclusion	I will just chalk this up to experience.
Action point	Perhaps I could find additional ways to motivate the girls.

Writing reflective accounts are a very good way to make sense of what has happened and to learn from experience. As the old adage states, 'one mind is better than two' and it is always helpful to talk to more experienced colleagues to gain their perspectives.

Learning from others

Schools often put in place formal mechanisms that are aimed to develop staff potential and professional development. As professionals involved in teaching and learning we often emphasise the importance of setting high expectations for the pupils we work with and that we need to communicate to them that we believe in them. Likewise, a Headteacher or line manager that genuinely believes that all staff members have the potential to be outstanding is more likely to bring out the best in those they work with. One TA reflects:

I remember working in a school where we all felt that whatever we did was just not good enough. But now I work at a school that feels completely different. One Wednesday a month, now referred to as, 'Wacky Wednesday', we are all encouraged to try something very different and creative within our class. It doesn't matter if the new ideas for learning that the teacher and I have come up with works or doesn't work ... it's a matter of trying new approaches, being creative and taking risks. In fact our school sees this as a way to encourage teachers/TAs to develop a growth mindset.

Effective schools believe in developing the potential for all staff and seek to encourage them to try out new ideas in a safe and respectful working environment. Ways of promoting professional development and learning include:

- Coaching – Drawing out solutions and encouraging self-awareness and reflection;
- Mentoring – Putting in, or recommending ideas and solutions;
- Active Listening – Acknowledgment of what the other has said in a caring and respectful manner.

Let's return to the example of Case Study 2.1, where Sadie describes her experiences with the Nightingale group with the school's Higher Level Teaching Assistant (HLTA), Jonie, from both a coaching and mentoring perspective.

Sadie says:	Jonie (HLTA) says wearing her MENTOR HAT	Jonie (HLTA) says wearing her COACHING HAT
I felt that I didn't handle the situation as well as I could have. I should have been able to motivate Daisy and Adele to work. Perhaps I could have found additional ways to motivate the girls.	I think you are spot on in thinking about trying to discover other ways to motivate the girls. I remember when I first starting working having difficulties motivating pupil like Daisy and Adele. What worked for me – was spending time with them discovering what their interests and hobbies were. I asked them what they did after school, on the weekend, what were their favourite shows, music, books and what they wanted to do when they grew up. Having this extra information enabled me to give them ideas. It is also important to be aware of gender stereotypes. There are many famous women explorers!	I think you are spot on in thinking about trying to discover other ways to motivate these pupils. When you are reluctant to do something what do *you* find helpful? What help, advice or guidance would *you* want from others? Would these approaches work with these pupils?

We can say from these specific examples that Jonie, as a Mentor gives specific advice and guidance and uses her expertise to help and guide Sadie.

However, Jonie, as the Coach is more non-directive, that is, she does not tell Sadie what to do but through effective questioning tries to get Sadie to think about what she is doing from different perspectives.

It is important to note that both these conversations are positive and supportive.

It is also important to remember that there is a time and place for both mentoring and coaching.

As one TA stated:

> When I first started working what I really needed was specific advice and top tips. Now however, I feel I benefit more from coaching conversations that really make me reflect on how and why I do things. But I also need to remember that when I am now working with new TAs that, what they need at least to begin with is clear and specific guidance.

Value of peer observation

There has been much written about the value of peer observation. Often the recommended first step is to decide on the focus of the observation. Various types of observations are illustrated in Table 2.1.

In today's world observation can also be virtual. Pearson et al. (2003) in an interesting study investigated the use of video material as a way to support and develop effective teacher/TA working relationships. Within this study classroom practice was filmed and the material viewed by both teachers and TAs together; this provided them with an opportunity to reflect together on what makes for outstanding practice.

Critical incidents

Within the literature reflection upon critical incidents is recommended as a way of enhancing self-knowledge. A critical incident can be a dramatic event, but more often is seen as a turning point, an event that has surprised you and that has led to some new understanding.

Table 2.1   Focus of peer observations

Focus of observation	What is observed	Examples of observation feedback
Experience of the learner	The observer is watching and making notes on how the pupils are responding to the session. The pupils' responses are then compared to the TA's intentions.	The TA intention was to have a group of four pupils engaged in writing a scary story together. The students were very interested but seemed to find it difficult to focus on the task. The students were almost too excited! Perhaps, more attention needed to be focused on structuring the task.
An aspect of practice the TA wishes to develop.	An aspect of practice is agreed before the observation and observation notes are made regarding how the TA engages with this aspect of practice.	The TA was interested in not only how she asked questions but whether there was a difference in the types of questions she asked pupils depending on their level of ability. The observer found that the TA tended to ask more challenging questions to the able students.
The observer gives their feedback from their perspective as a fellow teaching professional.	The observer, a fellow TA, would watch the session and make notes regarding how they would have both delivered and responded to the same learning situation. The difference in perspectives can offer both the observer and the observed new insights.	The TA observer, observed her fellow TA leading a reading intervention session. Though the TA observer also led reading intervention sessions it was interesting to note and discuss their different approaches to working with this same group of children.

In understanding the value of reflecting on critical events the following quote is helpful.

> Critical incidents are not things that exist independently of an observer and are awaiting discovery like gold nuggets on desert islands, but like all data, critical incidents are created. Incidents happen but critical incidents are produced by the way we look at a situation.
>
> (Tripp, 1993, p. 8)

So critical incidents are incidents that become critical through analysis and reflection; critical incidents come to challenge our ways of thinking and create opportunities for new understandings and knowledge. As one TA commented:

> This was not a life shattering dramatic moment but it did make a real difference to how I ask questions. I was working with a mixed ability group of students and we were discussing their up and coming science project. As I said it was a mixed ability group and most needed to be really encouraged to contribute to discussions – that is – with the exception of Ellie. Ellie is on the gifted and talented register. However, after one session Ellie was in tears and I asked her to stay behind. Ellie stated that she felt she was now the *class geek* and that no one liked her. I realised then – that my dependence on asking Ellie questions and praising Ellie for her thoughtful responses had somehow made the other students and Ellie perceive herself as being different. Obviously I changed my approach and the group works much better together now and of course Ellie is so much happier. But what that moment taught me was that I was looking at the session from my perspective rather than the pupils. It was a humbling to realise that I got it so wrong – but that moment, actually seven years ago – has changed the way I support pupils learning!

Discussion point

Critical incidents

Can you think of a critical incident that has made a difference to your practice?

Joint practice development

An interesting innovation in professional learning involves what is referred to as joint practice development. Hargreaves (2011, p. 10) contrasts a *knowledge model* of professional development where the emphasis is on studying formal literature and academic theory versus a *practice model*, where the focus is on learning by doing.

Hargreaves (2011) contrasts the peer-to-peer approach of 'sharing good practice' where educational professionals aim to tell other professionals about a practice that is both interesting and seems to work in their school to 'practice transfer'. Practice transfer as the name implies means that this new idea or new way of working is actually implemented within a new setting, i.e. a school or classroom. While sharing stories of good practice is incredibly valuable the limitation is the difficulty in translating a great idea into your own classroom with your pupils. Hargreaves (2011, p. 11) therefore argues that what is really needed are for educational professionals to, 'take responsibility for ensuring real practice transfer and being accountable if the practice is not really transferred'. So joint practice development involves practice transfer; but what does this mean? Well, it starts with mutual observation and coaching where new ideas are shared. Real practice transfer involves the person who has the great idea, or who has been recognised for some aspect of their great practice, going into another classroom and being responsible for working with the teacher/teaching assistant in that classroom to implement the new ideas in the new setting.

Case study 2.2: Joint practice development

Mrs Smith, the Headteacher, arranges an In-Service Training Day (INSET) day on the use of questioning to improve pupils' thinking skills. All of the TAs attend and the information is very interesting, useful and there were some great ideas. However, at the end of the day, many of the TAs said that they were not sure how to make it work in their classrooms with their pupils.

Mrs Smith, the Headteacher, decides to try out **joint practice development**. Mrs Smith knows that Amanda, the TA in Year 5, has a real flair for using questions to develop higher order thinking skills. The Headteacher encourages all the TAs to spend some time in Amanda's class in order to watch and learn. The TAs all value watching Amanda but are still not sure how to make it work in their classrooms with their pupils. At this point the Headteacher says, 'well observation is just the first step'.

The Headteacher asks Amanda to work in a number of other classrooms to share her great practice with others. Amanda works in a number of other classrooms with other TAs and helps them to develop their questioning skills. The other TAs feel that they now know what to do in their classrooms and Amanda feels that she has also learnt more about how to develop thinking skills through the use of questioning across all year groups.

Therefore joint practice is not just a matter of practice transfer, the expert showing the novice what to do, important as that can be. Rather, joint practice development involves both the giver and the receiver being involved in mutual observation where practice is not only shared but there is discussion on how practice can best be implemented in different settings and, therefore, both the giver and the receiver are learning. Joint practice development will be discussed further in Chapter 8.

Professional development

There have been many definitions regarding continuous professional development (CPD), though in terms of an overview it is helpful to acknowledge Eraut's (1994) view of CPD as all further learning which contributes to how a professional thinks and acts at work. Learning opportunities for TAs would include:

- External courses (apprenticeships, National Vocational Qualifications, Foundation degrees);
- Local Authority Training Days (for example a training day on, 'Supporting struggling readers');
- TA conferences;
- INSET days at school;
- Work-based opportunities (coaching, mentoring, shadowing colleagues, visiting other schools).

As an aspiring brilliant TA you need to participate in CPD and assist with CPD activities for new TAs.

What other TAs say

In this chapter we have talked about ways to become brilliant but perhaps it is best to leave the final word to the TAs we surveyed in regard to what they think makes for 'brilliance'.

Activity 2.3 What makes for a brilliant TA?

Either individually or in groups with other TAs, agree on 9 qualities that you believe are essential for a Brilliant TA. Once you have decided on these 9 qualities please rank them 'in a diamond 9' shape as shown in **Figure 2.2a**.

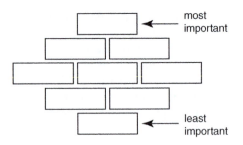

Figure 2.2a What makes for a great TA.

In a true 'Blue Peter' fashion we have tried this activity with TAs, who were on a Foundation degree, as part of the research for this book and what follows is their ideas (Figure 2.2b). It is important to realise that there are no right or wrong answers to this question, but what is important is to be able to argue why you feel certain traits or abilities are more important than others. Why do you think these TAs decided on the following? What do you think are the 9 qualities essential for being a brilliant TA and why?

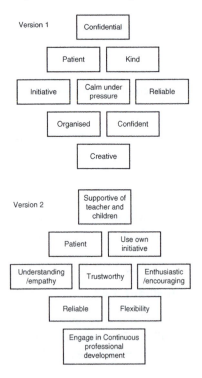

Figure 2.2b What makes for a great TA.

Summary

In this chapter we have talked about what makes for a brilliant TA and that becoming a brilliant TA is never an end point but an ever-continuing journey. However in saying that, this chapter has included many suggestions to help you on this journey to include: the use of reflection, having critical friends, mentors and the value of peer observation. Remember, a brilliant TA can change a pupil's life!

Chapter 3

The essentials

Introduction

At the beginning of your journey to become a brilliant teaching assistant there are essential pieces of knowledge that you need to be aware of. Although, you will bring your own personality, skills and attributes to the school, you will also need knowledge of the organisational framework that you work within to inform your daily practice. This chapter concerns essential information about two inter-related areas: **ethos** and **policies**.

When referring to ethos, we are specifically talking about the school ethos and **values** and how these support and underpin day-to-day inter-actions. Similarly, when discussing policies we are referring to school policies that contain key information and guidance which reflect the ethos of the school. School policies are informed by government legislation, reports and guidance, some of which we discussed in Chapter 1. As a TA, you will need to know how these policies impact your role and how to implement them when required. Coming to terms with the requirements of the school ethos and understanding the information and guidance within numerous policies that exist within a school may seem like a big ask. However line managers and mentors are there to help and it is their responsibility to ensure that TAs have read and understood essential school policies.

What do we mean by a school ethos?

Ethos can be defined as the characteristic spirit of a school as reflected in its attitudes and aspirations. Other words that can be used within schools to express this notion of ethos could include character and atmosphere. Nowhere can ethos be seen more clearly than through vision statements and school aims. Table 3.1 gives a few examples of such vision statements; however the challenge for the school is how to make these aspirations come alive in everyday interactions.

Table 3.1 Statements reflecting school ethos and values

Ethos or values

Our school is supported by the local Diocese. This means following Christian
values, chosen by the children. We use them to support our behaviour policy
and underpin the curriculum. These values include love and friendship, peace,
faith, forgiveness and respect.

Our school is a place to fulfil dreams. Our school has high expectations and is
committed to ensuring that all our pupils reach their potential. We have a
stimulating learning environment, a relevant and challenging curriculum and an
active partnership with families and the communities in which our pupils live,
work and play.

As a Rights Respecting School, the United Nations Convention on the Rights of the
Child, informs all that we do; it gives students a sense of purpose and develops
moral reasoning and an understanding of their place in the global community.

Discussion point

Living the vision statement

How could the values presented in Table 3.1 be implemented
day-to-day?

What is your school's vision statement and how is this implemented on a day-to-day level?

Where do policies come from?

It is important to understand that part of the ongoing process of
change in our schools is the result of government policy and changes
in our laws. The Department for Education offers advice to the governing schools bodies regarding the documents and policies that they
are required to hold. Further, these documents and policies will need
to be reviewed and updated in line with changing government legislation. Schools need to work within the law and policies of the government in power. As a TA you will feel the impact of these changes as
these laws and policies will directly affect the way you work in school.

However, it is important to note that there are opportunities for
schools and other stakeholders to make their views known when legislation concerning education is being developed. Consultations take
place regularly, for example parental views were taken into consideration when drafting legislation for the Special Educational Needs and
Disability Code of Practice: 0–25 years (DfE, DoH, 2015).

Pupils within the school can have a good introduction to the demo-
cratic process through consultation. For example, pupils are regularly

consulted through class councils, school councils and local authority questionnaires regarding their experience of school. Surveys such as Hampshire County Council's (2017) 'What do I think?' is given to all children in Years 2, 6, 7 and 9. This survey asks questions about personal and social aspects of school, behaviour, substance use and feeling safe in school. The data collected from such surveys can inform both the individual schools in improving the experience for their pupils and the local authority in planning professional development for teachers and governors.

Discussion point

Making your voice heard

As TAs you have an important contribution to make and you need to be aware of ways in which your voice can be heard.

What are the mechanisms for sharing your opinions about policy and practice in your setting?

What mechanisms should there be?

Values

Fundamental British values

Before we explore how schools develop their individual values we should consider the concept of 'fundamental British values (FBV). As part of the Teacher's Standards teachers are required,

> to uphold public trust in the profession and maintain high standards of ethics and behaviour, within and outside school. This includes not undermining fundamental British values.
>
> (DfE 2014, p. 5)

Teaching of these values through spiritual, moral, social and cultural (SMSC) education that the school provides must be seen to be robust. Schools that are not seen to promote FBV will be unable to get a good grade from Ofsted.

The concept of FBV is new, there has never before been a duty to teach a particular set of values in schools. The term FBV entered policy discourse in 2011, as part of the Home Office deliberations about the nature and prevention of violent terrorism and was used first in the 2012 Teacher's Standards and in 2014 in guidance for all schools (Richardson and Bolloten, 2015).

Fundamental British values are defined as 'democracy, the rule of law, individual liberty and mutual respect for and tolerance of those with different faiths and beliefs and for those without faith' (DfE 2014, p. 5). Some schools choose to refer to the values as 'human' or 'universal values' rather than as narrowly 'British' as they acknowledge that the majority of people would adopt theses values and the term British can be seen as exclusionary.

Case study 3.1: How our school teaches fundamental British values

Jayne is a TA in a small rural primary school and as Jayne explains:

In our school we had a whole school training day on how to promote fundamental British values as part of spiritual, moral, social and cultural (SMSC) education. Before training some of the TAs felt that this was just another directive to add to our workload and not very relevant to children in our rural primary school, where most of the children are white British and Christian or not of any faith.

We had a display in the corridor with a list of the fundamental British values and some flags and traditional British activities like Morris dancing and summer fetes. We also had pictures of the Queen, Buckingham Palace and food items such as a roast dinner and fish and chips. After the training it became clear that we needed to prepare our pupils to live in a diverse country and just because our school does not have a mixture of faiths and ethnicity it does not mean we don't need to teach our pupils about wider society. We audited our current opportunities to promote the values and found that there were many already such as: circle time; assemblies; topic work and stories and texts around aspects of diversity. Further, our school council provides an introduction to democracy. In class discussions we use examples of charitable giving to discuss issues of how people with disabilities or from different cultures are portrayed. As a staff team we reflected on the stories and texts we used in school and decided to ensure that they reflected our diverse society more accurately in terms of religion, sexuality and disability. The training raised our awareness that we live in a diverse society and that every child should have the opportunity to discuss and debate issues around diversity in an open and supported manner.

As TAs we realised that we have a duty to promote the values throughout the school day and to raise children's awareness of what being a good citizen in modern Britain involves.

Schools can promote fundamental British values (FBV) by including them in a coherent whole-school approach to spiritual, moral, social and cultural (SMSC) education, linking SMSC to school ethos and values and acknowledging that SMSC is wider and deeper than 'British values'.

School vision and ethos

Having considered the values to which all schools must adhere we now explore individual schools' values and how TAs can promote them. As we will see this is a process with a number of steps.

First impressions count

Every school has its own identity. When entering a school for the first time visitors very soon get an impression of what the school is like. The reception area and way that you are greeted often sets the tone of the school. Displays and signs around the school may indicate attitudes to equality and diversity. Levels of noise and engagement in classrooms give a flavour of the working atmosphere. Working atmosphere is also demonstrated through the manner in which staff, including TAs, interact with each other and with the pupils. Many schools prominently display their aims and values.

Discussion point

First impressions

When you have visited schools perhaps prior to an interview or as a parent – what were your first impressions?

How quickly did it take you to reach these impressions? On what basis did you make these impressions? What can you learn from this?

Knowing your aims and objectives

Becoming familiar with the school's aims and objectives is important. These are decided by senior leaders and staff, or by the whole school and are agreed with the governing body. The aims are published on the school website and in the prospectus. The ethos of the school in respect to issues such as inclusion, emotional wellbeing, the learning environment and relationships between home and school are expressed within the school aims. When joining a school TAs become ambassadors and it is their duty to share that ethos and vision. Schools' aims include phrases such as:

- To help children develop lively and enquiring minds;
- To be a community learning hub;
- That learning is high quality, and lessons are fun, with teachers making the best use of recent research to help them plan and deliver the best learning opportunities;
- To help children acquire knowledge and skills;
- To enable children to communicate effectively;
- To encourage tolerance and respect for others.

From aims to values

From their aims the staff and pupils of many schools have developed a set of values. Values are principles that underlie behaviour. Values influence both our actions and attitudes to ourselves and others and provide a framework for interactions with other people. Schools may agree to adopt a set of values such as compassion, creativity, respect, equality and collaboration. Some schools may phrase their values in 'child speak' to inspire pupils for example:

- Aiming high;
- Doing your best;
- Caring for the environment;
- Caring for each other.

Living the values

Values can be demonstrated in numerous ways from underpinning a nurturing 'classroom climate', through behaviour policies that focus on character development to supporting curriculum development. Sharing, demonstrating and modelling school values is an integral part of the work of all staff. Explicitly using the common language of the chosen values helps children to develop better social skills, become more reflective and feel part of a community. Research shows that pupils *in schools which hold a strong and well applied values based approach* show clear improvements in emotional stability, behaviour, attainment and awareness of the wider community (Farrer, 2010).

Case-study 3.2: How I communicate our values

Deepak is a TA in an urban primary school in a southern city and as Deepak explains: 'I worked in a Year 6 class this year. My school has a *Rights Respecting School Award* and its values system is based on the *United Nations Convention on the Rights of the Child.* We do not have special lessons on this but the values of the Convention run through everything we do. We use the language of rights respecting education as this helps develop pupils' acceptance of difference and diversity and helps them to develop a moral framework. Some of our pupils do not seem to get much support at home and some pupils come from homes that promote values at odds with the school. By demonstrating values in the way we speak and behave with colleagues and pupils and emphasising that rights apply to all pupils we hope to help the children develop as citizens. In my class there are a number of children who have behaviour challenges. We feel that 'keeping the school values in mind' is helpful when reminding children about behaving well. This means we all say the same sort of things to the pupils and relate to them in the same positive way.'

What 'kind of things' do you think Deepak and her colleagues were saying to pupils?

Many schools incorporate school values into their curriculum planning. Your setting may have an emphasis on outdoor learning and the environment, or on learning through play or collaboration through group work. Being aware of how school values influence the curriculum is key. A school that has 'care of the environment' as a core value will ensure that this is included in all areas of planning and strive to be 'eco-friendly' in the everyday practices of staff and pupils.

Many TAs live in the local community and as representatives of the school are sometimes seen as being more accessible for some parents than the teachers. TAs may be a first point of contact for families and it is important that the TAs support the school proactively in sharing the school's ethos and values with parents and pupils.

Safeguarding

We have previously discussed that school policies are developed as a result of responding to law and government policy. One of the main areas where this can be clearly seen is in keeping children safe in school.

The safety of pupils is paramount and all school staff need to contribute to building an atmosphere where children feel that school is a safe place, where they can grow and thrive. Safeguarding has a broader meaning than the procedures for protecting children who are at risk of harm or abuse. Safeguarding is proactive.

As such, safeguarding and promoting the welfare of children is defined by the DfE (2016) as:

- protecting children from maltreatment;
- preventing impairment of children's health or development;
- ensuring that children grow up in circumstances consistent with the provision of safe and effective care;
- taking action to enable all children to have the best outcomes.

(Dfe 2016, p.5)

'Child protection' relates to the procedures that are used to protect children if abuse or neglect is suspected. TAs need to be clear about their roles in both instances. All members of staff should receive safeguarding training that includes understanding child protection procedures. In the year 2013/2014 over 650,000 children in England were referred to local authority children's social care services by individuals who had concerns about their welfare (DfE, DoH, 2015, p. 7). Government guidelines confirm that:

safeguarding and promoting the welfare of children is everyone's responsibility. Everyone who comes into contact with children and their families and carers has a role to play in safeguarding children.

(DfE, 2016, p. 5)

A child-centred approach is advocated where the guiding principle is always to do what is in the best interest of the child. It is important to remember that for children who are vulnerable, every day matters. Academic research is consistent in stressing the damage to children that occurs from delaying intervention. 'The actions taken by professionals to meet the needs of these children as early as possible can be critical to their future' (DfE, DoH, 2015 p. 7).

A multi-agency approach is essential when working to protect a child. Education, Health and Children and Young Peoples services have a statutory duty to work together. Coordinating this work is the Local Safeguarding Children Boards (LSCBs) in each area. LSCBs are made up of local services and organisations working with children for example, police, youth justice, education, health and children and adult services.

Every school has a designated safeguarding/child protection person; often several members of staff within a school take on this responsibility. You should ensure that you know whom to approach in the event of any concerns.

Being vigilant

TAs are often very well placed to observe children both in class, in the playground and around the school. Busy teachers who are delivering the curriculum, organising the class and assessing learning may sometimes be less well placed than their TAs to notice small changes in behaviour that may indicate that a child is anxious or in distress. It is acknowledged that no single professional can have a full picture of a child's needs and circumstances and it is the duty of all who come into contact with children and their families to keep children's best interests at heart (DfE 2016). TAs who support pupils at lunchtime may notice children who have inadequate food in their lunch boxes or who are always hungry. TAs may also notice changes in patterns of behaviour, for example reluctance to come into school, disengagement with the curriculum, becoming agitated at home time or spending time alone in the playground which may be unusual. TAs are advised to use playtimes and lunch times to interact with pupils and to be observant of all the children. Noticing and preventing bullying is also an important part of safeguarding children. TAs may notice physical signs of abuse, bruising or be aware when children have problems with hygiene. Being alert, noting and sharing these observations can be essential in helping to build a profile of a child who may otherwise go unnoticed.

Children's views

When children and young people were asked what teachers should do to keep children safe they said:

- check that children are eating at school and aren't too hungry;
- talk to parents and build a relationship with them;
- don't tell the parents what a child has said – it could make things worse;
- be someone they can trust;
- don't tell other teachers what they've told you;
- be someone that deals with it straight away, not six days later;

- be careful how you word things – don't annoy parents the child has to go home to;
- look for children who are withdrawn or who start bullying others.

(DfE, 2013, p. 22)

Children may be concerned about confidentiality and as the above research suggests children may ask that you don't tell their parents or other teachers what they have said. **However, and this is very important, children and young people need to understand that information will be shared on a need-to-know basis and that you cannot keep secrets.** You should always make children and young people aware of whom you need to tell.

There are four main categories of abuse. These are **emotional abuse, sexual abuse, physical abuse and neglect.**

Discussion point

What do I need to know?

With a colleague access the National Society for the Prevention of Cruelty to Children information online about child abuse found at https://www.nspcc.org.uk/preventing-abuse/signs-symptoms-effects/
Ensure that you are familiar with the categories and the signs of abuse.

Dangers that children may face include: staying safe online; joining gangs; using illegal drugs or alcohol. The schools' *Personal, Social, Health and Citizenship* education and *Spiritual, Moral, Social and Cultural* programmes should incorporate discussing these potential risks and recognise that there are many children who are vulnerable to outside influences and social and cultural pressures.

Responding to disclosures

A TA may be the person a child trusts; therefore a child may feel comfortable in disclosing to the TA issues of abuse or neglect. As part of your induction senior leaders will brief you on what to do if a child makes a disclosure to you. There are some essential principles to keep in mind if this occurs:

- Go slowly, take your time both in terms of talking and listening to the child;

- Do not ask leading questions or 'interview' the child;
- Make an accurate written note of the conversation you have had with the child on a concern sheet as soon as you can;
- Accept that what the child says is true;
- Never promise to keep anything the child tells you a secret. They need to understand that you have to pass on what they have said and that it will be dealt with sensitively;
- Tell them what will happen next as far as you can;
- When completing a concerns sheet keep it factual – do not put your own interpretation onto what they have told you. If unsure, talk to your teacher or senior leader regarding how to complete the 'concern sheet'.

Case study 3.3: Following procedures

Olivia is a TA in a school in a leafy suburb. The staff has received safeguarding training, however Olivia does not expect any of the pupils she works with to have any problems in this area. She believes that it is 'after all an affluent area and things like that don't usually happen here'.

Lisa is a quiet child with a small circle of friends. Olivia has a good relationship with Lisa and works in a literacy catch-up intervention with her twice a week. In the playground Lisa seems distressed. Olivia goes to ask her what is wrong and Lisa won't answer. Later that day Lisa seeks Olivia out and says she doesn't want to go home. Her dad has been hurting her. She shows Olivia a bruise on her arm; the finger marks are clear. Olivia reassures Lisa and does not question her further. Olivia makes a note of what she has said and quickly passes this information on to the designated safeguarding person, in this case the Headteacher. Children and Young People's Services are called and Lisa is not allowed to go home with her mother.

The Headteacher praises Olivia for following procedures correctly. However, at home that evening Olivia is anxious and concerned for Lisa and her family. She finds it hard to accept what Lisa has told her in the context of what she knows about the family. What if she shouldn't have passed the information on? What if the family blame her for what happens next? What if Lisa is lying? Olivia understands that she cannot discuss this confidential issue with her husband. She has a sleepless night.

The next day at school the Headteacher asks Olivia how she is feeling and Olivia discusses her anxieties. The Headteacher reassures Olivia that she did the right thing and acted in the best interests of the child. The Headteacher offers continuing support for Olivia and an opportunity to speak with the local authority counselling team.

Olivia continues to feel anxious, but when she is made aware of the outcomes for Lisa and her family, she knows that she did the right thing. Olivia reflected on her assumption that abuse and neglect were unlikely in her school and now realises that this can happen in any setting and decides to be more vigilant in future.

Prevent

The Prevent duty can be viewed as one of the measures schools take to keep their pupils safe from harm. It is the duty required by the Counter-Terrorism and Security Act (DfE, 2015) and authorities such as schools and child care providers need to be aware that they have a specific duty of care to prevent people from being drawn into terrorism. This Act has drawn criticism from some (Ramsay, 2017) as it is believed to be biased against Muslim organisations. However, the Act refers to all types of terrorist groups including right wing groups and animal rights groups, who use violent means, as well as radical Islamist groups. Any organisation that is likely to attempt indoctrination through propaganda techniques, family or peer pressure, social media or websites that may lead children or young people to harm themselves or others comes under the scope of the Prevent duty. Teaching 'fundamental British values' and encouraging pupils of all ages to develop critical thinking is part of the strategy to enable children and young people to resist extremist ideology. Teachers are encouraged to engage pupils in critical thinking about all the issues that may lead vulnerable pupils into joining any kind of extremist organisation that promotes intolerance and violence. Please do talk to your teacher if you have any concerns. Schools will be working in different contexts and the likelihood of different kinds of radicalisation will vary from locality to locality. Primary schools and early years providers need to remember that, 'even very young children may be vulnerable to radicalisation by others, whether in the family or outside, and display concerning behaviour' (DfE, 2015, p. 6). Schools will use the *same safeguarding strategies* and procedures to support pupils at risk of radicalisation as for other types of issues such as abuse, drug taking etc. Remember always speak to your designated child protection/safeguarding lead if you have any concerns.

Discussion point

What would you do?

Discuss with your colleagues the steps you would take in the following scenario.

Karl is a Year 6 pupil who joined the school at the beginning of the September term. He has had difficulty making friends and has made some unkind comments about pupils with special educational needs, which you discussed with him. Karl shows little understanding or remorse and has been aggressive and sulky in his response. Today, though you couldn't hear the words he used but from his tone of voice you think he may have used racist language to a Polish pupil during a football match. The boy, who received these comments, will not tell you what was said. He seems scared of Karl and doesn't want to be involved. There have been attacks on some Polish teenagers in the town by a right wing group.

How would you follow this up given the heightened tension in the community?

Confidentiality

TAs have the same duty as teachers to support the school by always being appropriate in their conversations with parents and people in the community. TAs should be discreet in their conversations about individual pupils and never reveal information they may know from administrative tasks such as filing reports or through attendance at meetings, or information passed on to them on *a need to know basis*. Discussing SATs results or Ofsted information before it is publicly available would be unacceptable. If parents have confidential issues they wish to discuss, you will need to refer them to teachers or senior leaders. It is important to protect yourself by keeping your own personal contact information confidential and never to discuss school issues on social media such as Facebook.

Health and safety

Pupils with conditions such as epilepsy, arthritis, severe allergic conditions, heart conditions or asthma need to access as much of the curriculum as possible. They need a health care plan and TAs may be asked to administer medication, but cannot be required to if they are not happy to do so. In your role as a TA if you agree to carry out procedures such as administering drugs or catheterisation, for pupils with continence issues, you will need to know the Department for Education advice contained in the statutory guidance, 'Supporting pupils with medical conditions at school' (DfE, 2014). If this is part of your role the school will arrange training in the procedures for administering medication or other forms of support, usually by a school nurse or other health care professionals. Details of healthcare plans should be shared on a *need to know* basis and kept confidential.

All staff will receive fire safety training. Make sure you know how to use fire extinguishers and blankets and where they are located. Support your class teacher in keeping fire exits clear in classrooms and ensuring you know the exit route for wheelchair users in every classroom you work in, as part of your inclusive practice. Know where the class assembly point is located for fire drills and that correct routes have suitable access for all pupils. Use your common sense to be aware of hazards in and around the school and report any that you find.

Online safety

Schools need robust and constantly updated online safety policies and procedures to safeguard children and protect them from bullying on social media, grooming and also the effects of watching pornography or playing excessively violent games online. In school materials are screened and there are controls in place. However, pupils may often be one step ahead in understanding and using technology than those who are instructing them. All staff are required to sign the *Staff Acceptable Use Policy* which outlines the purposes and systems of how staff may use online information. Ensure that you are familiar with your school's policy and practice guidance and that you report any concerns to the safeguarding lead. Be careful in your own use of social media outside of school. Digital communications with students via email, text or Virtual Learning Environment (VLE) should be on a professional level and only carried out using official school systems. This is for your protection as well as the pupils.

Sexting, which is the posting and sharing of sexual imagery, has become worryingly prevalent among young people in recent years. Research on the prevalence of sexting has suggested that between 15 and 40 per cent of pupils had been involved in some level of 'sexting' behaviour (Ringrose et al., 2012). Government and DfE approved guidance to support schools is contained in the document, 'Sexting in schools and colleges: Responding to incidents and safeguarding young people' (UKCCIS, 2017). Advice from the NSPCC states that while,

> sexting can be seen as harmless, creating or sharing explicit images of a child is illegal, even if the person doing it is a child. A young person is breaking the law if they: take an explicit photo or video of themselves or a friend; share an explicit image or video of a child, even if it's shared between children of the same age; or possess, download or store an explicit image or video of a child, even if the child gave their permission for it to be created.
>
> (NSPCC, 2018)

The correct terminology is 'youth-produced sexual imagery' and although this breaks the law, 'as of January, 2016, in England and Wales if a young person is found creating or sharing images the police can choose to record that a crime has been committed but that taking formal action isn't in the public interest' (NSPCC, 2018).

If you became aware of such an incident, then in your role as a TA, you would need to refer this to the designated safeguarding lead (DSL). In many cases images can be deleted and the incident dealt with in school (UKCCIS, 2017). However if the incident involves an adult, coercion, suspected grooming, or any concerns about the pupil's capacity to consent for example through language difficulties or any worrying sexual behaviour, then outside agencies including the police should be notified (UKCCIS, 2017).

You need to be aware of e-safety issues related to the use of mobile phones, cameras and handheld devices and monitor their use. If you are Information Communication Technology (ICT) 'phobic' you must gain support to be sure that you know enough to carry out these actions. Request support or training if you need to. Brilliant TAs are proactive in seeking development and training opportunities!

Legislation

At the beginning of the chapter we stated that the Department for Education offers advice to the governing bodies of schools regarding the documents and policies that they are required to hold. Further, these documents and policies will need to be reviewed and updated in line with changing government legislation. In this section we aim to explore two important Acts that are examples of legislation that influence our practice every day; they are the **'Equality Act 2010'** and the **'Children and Families Act 2014'**.

The **Equality Act** describes how we should treat other people in order to avoid discrimination. The Act lists the groups which are covered by the legislation as having 'protected characteristics' which include age, disability, gender reassignment, marriage and civil partnership, pregnancy and maternity, race, religion or belief, sex and sexual orientation. For schools and other public bodies there is a duty to abide by the Equality Act. Information regarding how this should be met is outlined in the Public Sector Equality Duty Guidance for Schools in England (EHRC, 2014).

> Compliance with the equality duty is a legal requirement, but meeting it also makes good education sense. The equality duty helps schools to focus on key issues of concern and how to improve pupil outcomes.
>
> (EHRC, 2014, p. 5)

Issues of concern referred to in this guidance include: performance gaps between groups of pupils, ensuring all pupils can participate in school activities and engage effectively in learning. Schools should ensure that pupils are not bullied or discriminated against. The Stonewall School Report (Stonewall, 2017, p. 4) shows that though anti-lesbian, gay, bisexual, transgender (LGBT) bullying and language has decreased across Britain's schools since 2012 still almost half of all LGBT pupils face bullying at school for being LGBT, and more than two in five trans young people have tried to take their own life. This is clearly unacceptable.

TAs and other staff working in schools should ensure that they are working in accordance with the Equality Act. As a TA, your role is to promote an appreciation of diversity, and to encourage pupils to demonstrate both empathy and understanding.

Discussion point

Complying with the Equality Act

How does my school comply with the Equality Act?

We asked a group of Foundation students, how their school complied with the Equality Act. Their responses were as follows:

Parent support classes – including language classes
Homework support
Books in different languages
Wheelchair access

Learning mentors

Using a variety of images in lessons showing different ethnicity, people with disabilities, showing both sexes in roles at work and in the home

Display boards and books of 'My Family' which reflect diverse images of family life

Use of signing such as Makaton

Provision of a prayer room

Providing spaces and activities for children who do not access assembly and festivals because of their religion

Texts reflecting different cultures

Supporting pupils with gender identity issues

Exploring different religions and beliefs

Staff training on equality issues

As a TA how do you think the responses above could be used to promote empathy and understanding?

The next essential piece of legislation to change school practice is the Children and Families Act (2014) which addresses areas such as adoption, child welfare, parental leave, rights to flexible working and family justice. For schools the key area for consideration is Part 3 of the Act, which refers to reforms to provision and practice in the Special Educational Needs and Disability (SEND) section. This legislation in turn led to the development of the Special Educational Needs Code of Practice: 0–25 years (DfE, DoH, 2015).

Special educational needs and disability

The designation of Special Educational Needs occur:

> when a child or young person has a learning difficulty or a disability and they need to have special educational provision made for them. This means where a child has any educational provision which is additional to or different from that generally given to other pupils of the same age.
>
> (Children and Families Act 2014, pp. 15–16)

This revised Code (DfE, DoH, 2015) emphasises the importance of the voice of the pupil and parents in decision making and planning, and brought in a single category of **SEND Support**, replacing School Action

Table 3.2 Areas of need

Area of Need	To include:
Cognition and learning	Moderate learning difficulties (MLD), severe learning difficulties (SLD) through to profound and multiple learning difficulties (PMLD); Specific learning difficulties that affect one or more areas of learning such as dyslexia, dyspraxia and dyscalculia.
Social, emotional and mental health	Difficulties in this area may manifest itself in a number of ways to include pupils being withdrawn, isolated, displaying challenging or disruptive behaviour. Such behaviours may reflect anxiety or depression, self-harming, substance misuse or eating disorders. Some pupils may be diagnosed as having attention deficit disorder, attention deficit hyperactive disorder or attachment disorder.
Sensory and/or physical needs	Visual or hearing impairment, multi-sensory impairment or physical disability.
Communication and interaction	Speech and language difficulties, (delays and disorders); Children and young people with Autism or Autism Spectrum Disorders (ASD), and Asperger's Syndrome may have specific difficulties with social interaction.

and School Action plus (from the previous SEN Code of Practice, 2001). A pupil is seen to be in need of SEND support if the school feels that they need more than 'quality first teaching' to ensure good progress. Here quality first teaching is defined as the appropriate use of strategies to include questioning, modelling, explaining and learning through dialogue. **Education, Health and Care Plans** (EHCP) replaced the Statements of Educational needs for those children with the most complex needs. Another key improvement to the Code (2015) is that it now covers the years 0-25 and as such meets the needs of the youngest as well as improving provision for college-age students.

The Code divides SEND into four main broad areas of need (See Table 3.2). However, it is important to note that children's needs may not fit neatly into these categories and individual profiles should be drawn up for each child.

Responsibilities

The SEND Code (DfE, DoH, 2015) emphasises the class teacher's role in taking responsibility for the learning of all the pupils in the class. Many TAs in past years, as we have outlined in Chapter 1, have been directed to work only with lower ability groups and have provided the majority of support in core subjects for these pupils. However the Code *now* states that:

> Teachers are responsible and accountable for the progress and development of the pupils in their class, including where pupils access support from teaching assistants or specialist staff.
>
> (DfE, DoH, 2015, p. 99)

Good practice occurs when the class teacher plans for and works with every child. In this case the TAs may be used to add value to what the teacher does. TAs need to work with all pupils and understand that they must promote pupil independence wherever possible, including for those pupils with SEND. Interventions are often led by TAs and occur outside of the classroom, though teachers should be aware of the ongoing progress of their pupils in planned interventions. Teachers are required to reinforce the learning that takes place within planned interventions within pupil work in the classroom; this therefore requires the teacher and TA to talk in detail about pupil progress. Communication between teachers and TAs needs to be planned and systematic (for further information see pp. 124–125). In the research carried out for this book TAs that were surveyed noted that working with 'teacher planned small groups on interventions' was the second most important part of their role, the first being, keeping pupils on task.

Education Health Care Plan (EHCP)

An EHCP is given as a result of a local authority *statutory assessment* involving parents, teachers, the SENCo and other professionals such as an educational psychologist (EP). The EHC needs assessment is normally not the first step in the process of planning support; rather, it follows on from previous planning and support that has already taken place. Schools will need to demonstrate both what they have already put in place to support the pupil's learning and the outcomes of this support in their request for statutory assessment. Of course an EHC needs assessment will not necessarily lead to an EHC plan; as 'information gathered during an EHC needs assessment may indicate ways in which the school, college or other provider can meet the child or young person's needs without an EHC plan' (DfE, 2015, p. 143).

The SEND Code of Practice (2015) specifies four key aspects to an EHC plan (section 9.2, p. 142):

- establish and record the views, interests and aspirations of the parents and child or young person;

- provide a full description of the child or young person's special educational needs and any health and social care needs;
- establish outcomes across education, health and social care based on the child or young person's needs and aspirations;
- specify the provision required and how education, health and care services will work together to meet the child or young person's needs and support the achievement of the agreed outcomes.

The graduated approach

The graduated approach is a model of action and intervention which aims to both remove barriers to learning and implement effective special educational provision. This action or support takes the form of a four-part cycle, consisting of Assess, Plan, Do and Review. This ongoing cycle involves the review of earlier decisions and actions, or cycles, in order to refine and revise provision with the aim of coming to a greater understanding of both individual need and the support required to make good progress. The cycle of action – **Assess, Plan, Do and Review** will involve TAs at some or all of the stages.

Assess

The class teacher and the SENCo will carry out an analysis to **assess** the pupil's needs. Parents views and experiences, the views of the child and, if relevant, advice from outside professionals or external support services will inform the assessment. TAs have their role to play as they may have in-depth knowledge of the pupil. Further TAs may be trained to undertake pupil assessments, for example in reading or maths or motor skills, the outcomes of which will inform the analysis of a pupil's need.

Plan

Teacher and SENCos in consultation with parents and children and young people will **plan** the required support that will include details of adjustments and interventions to be put into place. TAs may have input to planning programmes. All teachers, TAs and support staff working with pupils need to know details of the pupil's needs, outcomes and interventions and teaching strategies to be used. In order to communicate information schools may use pupil passports, individual learning plans, and group learning plans or individual provision maps. Pupil passports outline information about the pupil and are often written with the pupil.

They can provide information for staff working with the individual pupil and may outline useful ways to support the pupil, their likes and dislikes and interests or how to communicate effectively. Learning plans generally detail what the pupil needs to work on, who will provide support and when it will take place. There is no requirement to produce individual education programmes (IEPs), though schools must record their provision and progress made towards pupil learning outcomes.

Do

As a TA, you may be involved in the **do** stage by delivering interventions, scaffolding for learning and supporting pupils in class and supporting teachers to deliver individual programmes. You should receive training for these roles and have feedback from class teachers and SENCos to support your role. Specialist teachers may work with a child though class teachers must remain in overall charge of the programme and continue to work with all the pupils in the class, including those with SEN.

Review

A Review will be held, at an agreed time, to discuss the effectiveness of the support and interventions and the impact this has had on pupil progress. As a TA you will be involved in the **review** stage by feeding back to the class teacher information about progress made in interventions or sharing observations made in class. As a TA you may be asked to be part of planning and review meetings for the pupils in your class.

Case study 3.4: Being involved with EHCPs and the graduated approach

Dave is a TA in Year 4 in a mainstream school. He supports Leonie who is eight years old.

Assess

Leonie's assessment of need states that she has cerebral palsy which affects her left side and she is also on the autism spectrum. Leonie has some difficulty in negotiating smaller spaces in the classroom, although she can walk unaided. Leonie copes well in an uncluttered environment. Her balance is occasionally an issue. She dislikes change and can become agitated at unexpected events.

Plan

Dave prepared to work with Leonie by reading her EHCP, her pupil passport and Individual Learning Programme carefully. From reading these documents Dave knows that he needs to encourage Leonie to be independent in the classroom and adapt the environment to support this wherever possible. He knows he needs to make an extra effort to keep the classroom 'clutter free' and gangways accessible. He reads the teacher's planning carefully and checks that he knows exactly what to do and say.

Do

Dave knows that teachers are responsible and accountable for the progress and development of all pupils in their class, though Dave knows that he has an important role to play. Dave knows that ongoing communication with the teacher, SENCo and relevant outside agencies is crucial. Dave understands that Leonie needs to develop a strong relationship with the class and ensures that she is able to do this by encouraging and supporting Leonie to work with other children and groups. Dave's support for her is sensitive and not overbearing. Leonie has difficulty manipulating objects such as pencils, buttons and zips. He knows when to scribe for her and when to encourage her to write. Leonie is good at maths and needs little support other than occasionally to manipulate apparatus or equipment. Dave helps her to update her visual timetable and signals upcoming changes in routines for her clearly by explaining what will happen and when.

Review

Dave is also involved in updating Leonie's pupil passport. He notes success towards her learning targets and decides with her teacher when she has met them and helps to set new targets. He keeps notes to contribute to the Annual Review of her EHCP. He speaks with Leonie's parents regularly.

Dave is involved in all stages of the Graduated Approach, having explicit knowledge of this cycle helps him to work on agreed outcomes for Leonie throughout the school day.

Inclusive practice

Inclusion means more than meeting the needs of pupils with special needs and disabilities, although this is a major part of inclusive practice. There are many pupils who need both to be and to feel included. Schools can demonstrate their inclusivity by taking positive steps to support and provide provision for all pupils to include those from ethnic minorities, Gypsy Roma Travellers, pupils with English as an additional language, pupils who are lesbian, gay, bisexual or transgender and gifted and talented pupils. We have now returned again to the area of 'vision and values' that we discussed at the beginning of the chapter. Booth and Ainscow (2016) discuss many definitions of inclusive education, one of which is the simple definition that inclusive education supports everyone to feel that they belong. However, when we talk of belonging we need to make sure we listen to the voices of the pupils we work with. To what extent do they feel comfortable in the school and to what extent do they feel accepted and valued? Many schools are proud to consider themselves inclusive. However, inclusion is an ongoing process that is constantly changing as our society evolves.

Discussion point

Promoting inclusion

What makes for an inclusive school?

When asking our Foundation degree students how their setting promotes inclusion for pupils with SEND, TAs responded in a variety of ways.

Some replied that they were proud of their school's inclusive ethos, they never turned a child away, but looked for the best ways to help that child succeed. One TA wrote that, 'Our school staff are encouraged to be open minded and have an ethos that every child has a right to a place at our school. Extra help or support is given whether it be from SEND professionals (educational psychologists or speech and language therapists) or school staff.'

Strategies such as breakfast clubs, learning interventions and social and emotional support, extracurricular activities, differentiation and using resources that reflect a wide variety of backgrounds were seen as ways of meeting pupils' needs.

Some TAs linked their practice in SEND to wider school values and described promoting their school as a whole family, where everyone is accepted and valued.

What do you feel makes for an inclusive school?

Summary

This chapter has covered some essential issues in education. It may be possible to work efficiently as a TA without having had much consideration for wider social issues, government's legislation, policies and guidance that affect practice, school ethos, inclusive practice, issues around safeguarding or considering your own attitudes to equality and diversity. However if you have started the journey towards being a 'brilliant' TA it is important to reflect on these issues and consider your own attitudes and understand how they impact on your everyday practice. Evaluating the essentials will help you to grow as a TA and as a person. Taking time to see the big picture and step back from the day-to-day small incidents of school life will enable you to make significant steps on your journey to becoming a brilliant TA.

Chapter 4

Understanding learning

Introduction

Understanding how we learn has been the focus of interest to many philosophers, psychologists, behavioural scientists and teachers over the centuries. By 'learning' we mean how humans develop from helpless babies that require nurturing for longer than any other animal, into adults who have acquired skills and knowledge that enable them to achieve and thrive in a complex world. How do we do this? How can we help or enable others to learn? The answers to these questions are fundamental to what we do on a day-to-day basis in our classrooms.

Case study 4.1: On holiday

Whilst on holiday I watched toddlers and small children playing in a pool. The principles of learning were all encapsulated in this activity. What was happening that transformed these small land-based creatures into confident and competent water babies? Even toddlers who had only been walking for a few months made progress in their skills and confidence. They learned to jump in, go right under the water and surface laughing and spluttering. The children wanted to play and explore. Their motivation was high. The water was warm, the sun was shining and the pool was the right depth for children.

Supportive parents were giving full attention to their children. However, the parents only gave this attention when the children needed it. The rest of the time parents were happy for the children to explore and play as long as they could observe them and were close at hand in case they needed them. Parents in this case acted as a secure base. Parents gave lots of encouragement but put in boundaries where needed ('be careful not to splash the little ones'). Some parents who were working on teaching their children swimming modelled and demonstrated strokes. Parents provided support with armbands and rubber rings, and demonstrated how to use them. They gave lots of positive feedback and told their children what to do to improve – 'kick harder' or 'keep your head up.'

Personality and experience both played a part – some children were cautious and anxious when first entering the water while others seemed reckless. However, even the shyest child developed confidence with support from siblings and parents. As well as learning new skills in relation to swimming, social learning was taking place. Some children played together, some in parallel with others, some organised their games making new friends easily. A few children practised and persevered until they could swim unaided for short distances spurred on by admiration of the older children, their role models. Motivation and fun were key elements of what was happening. Conditions for learning were good!

Perhaps you too have similar memories from family holidays. As we progress through this chapter we will consider how these simple observations regarding how young children learnt to swim are reflected in explanations of learning.

On your journey to becoming a brilliant TA you will find that having some knowledge of learning theories can help you to make sense of what happens in the classroom and enable you to better support the children you work with. Teachers will have been taught theories of learning in their training, a knowledge of these key terms will help you to begin to engage in 'teacher speak.' The field of learning is vast and what will be covered in this chapter will be key concepts to cover the areas of:

- Intelligence and learning;
- Optimum conditions for learning;
- Cognitive learning theories;
- Neuroscience: how current knowledge of the brain is influencing our ideas about learning;
- Meta-cognition: the importance of pupils understanding how they learn and how they can improve their own learning;
- Working memory;
- Attachment: the interconnectedness of brain development and emotional nurturing;
- Language development.

Intelligence and learning

It is worth considering what we mean by intelligence. When we discuss intelligence we usually mean an individual's potential to learn things. When describing a child as intelligent we infer that we think they can learn things easily and remember more than some other children. The more intelligent they are the more quickly they will learn a wider range of subjects. The traditional view of 'intelligence' is that it is a 'single, measurable, inborn and unchangeable entity' (Jarvis, 2005, p. 43). This implies that intelligence is a 'standalone' factor not changed by circumstances or environment. You either have it or you don't. However this view of intelligence is seen as a very damaging and can lead to what Carol Dweck (2017) refers to as fixed mindset. We will talk much more about this in Chapter 7. Further, this notion that you 'either have it or you don't' does not take into account the effort that you put into a task, your perseverance when learning is challenging, your expectations regarding your ability to succeed and of course the learning environment. Most theorists, to include Vygotsky and Bruner, would argue that the context within which a child's learning takes place is crucial. Whilst some armchair theorists may argue that particular children may have innate predispositions for certain types of learning; that is, one child may have a gift for playing the violin or performing gymnastics, that is by no means the whole story. Adding to this debate on the nature of intelligence: Gardner (1983) has written on multiple intelligences; Goleman (1996) has discussed emotional intelligence and Carol Dweck (2017) has written extensively on the power of fixed and growth mindsets while Malcolm Gladwell, in his book *Outliers* (2008), argues that it takes roughly 10,000 hours of deliberate practice to become world-class in any field.

Discussion point

Ability, intelligence and expectations

How do you define ability? How do you define intelligence?
Which children in your class do you consider to be the most or least 'able'?
On what basis did you make this judgement?
Consider the way you interact with groups and individual pupils. Does your understanding of ability or intelligence and your expectations of what you think a child can achieve affect your interactions with them?
Have you ever felt that others have made judgements regarding your ability? How did this make you feel?

Optimum conditions for learning

If intelligence is not fixed and learning potential is affected by everything around us then we need to understand and be aware of the optimum conditions for learning and importantly how we can facilitate this in classrooms where we work. The development of a child is extremely complex and comparisons between children will reveal huge variations in development. Indeed Piaget argued that while all children go through the same stages of development they progress at a pace that is unique to them. For example a parent may say my oldest was talking fluently by 18 months while my youngest was still having difficulties in language when he started school; however both are now at university.

We often divide discussion of development in to social, emotional, physical and cognitive domains. These are convenient labels and make learning about human development more manageable however they are unreal divisions as each area influences development in other areas. It is important to see the interrelatedness of all these categories, that is, to take a holistic approach to human development.

Many factors influence learning. Biological and physiological factors such as sensory processing (having good sight, hearing etc.), genetic predispositions, good nutrition, adequate sleep or the effects of medical conditions will impact on a child's capacity to learn. Good language skills are associated with good thinking skills. Nurturing relationships with caregivers build strong brain networks in the developing child. A nurturing relationship provides an environment for emotional and social learning as well as supporting the development of language and cognitive skills. Emotional factors such as a child feeling that they are loved and valued leads to good mental health.

When we discuss a child's learning needs in school we are usually referring to their cognitive development. Have they met age-related expectations in varying areas of the curriculum? However, if a pupil is 'underachieving', that is, not reaching age related expectations, we need to look at all the factors that affect learning and specifically what the school can do to make a difference.

The social environment such as housing, family support and structure all play a crucial part in a child's development. Poverty or financial problems can add strain to family life and affect pupils learning. Parental attitudes to school and education will influence the support that pupils receive at home and consequently have an effect on a child's progress in school. Each child's potential to learn will be influenced by their own profile of attitudes, beliefs, social and emotional support, genetic and biological attributes, physiological needs and cognitive strengths and weaknesses. The interplay between these factors has been the subject of the 'nature versus nurture' debate, that is, which is more important your nature (genetic inheritance) or nurture (your environment)? A genetic condition, like Down syndrome may have a strong effect on a child's learning but the environment in terms of the love, support and encouragement that a child receives coupled with a good education can improve outcomes. Conversely, a child with a high level of cognitive ability may fail to make expected progress due to a problematic family background, poverty or other issues.

Case study 4.2: High expectations and enriched experiences can make a difference!

Reading instruction for children with Down syndrome – the Sarah Duffen Centre, Portsmouth

Historically, there have been very low academic expectations for children with Down syndrome. It was once thought that individuals with Down syndrome could not read and therefore they were not taught to read. However, a powerful example of how high expectations and an enriched environment can make a difference to learning is demonstrated by the work of Professor Sue Buckley, a leading researcher in the field. In 1979, Leslie Duffen contacted Sue Buckley about his daughter Sarah, who had Down syndrome, and had been making amazing progress at a mainstream school. Sara's exceptional progress was attributed to her early reading experience as Sarah had been introduced to reading from the age of 3 years. Leslie Duffen felt that his daughter had learned to talk from *seeing* language rather than *hearing* the language. Sue Buckley and colleagues began to research this area and indeed found that teaching a sight vocabulary to pre-schoolers with Down syndrome was both possible and beneficial to language and cognitive development. This formed the basis for successful practice with many children up to the present day.

(Buckley, 2002)

The beliefs we hold about the abilities of the children we support, that is, the expectations we have for them and likewise the hopes, or aspirations we hold for their futures are extremely powerful as classic research by Rosenthal and Jacobson (1966) demonstrated. In this classic study pupils were given an intelligence test at the beginning of the year and teachers were informed of the names of pupils who the test deemed to be 'academic bloomers.' At the end of the year all pupils were again given intelligence tests and sure enough those who had been identified as academic bloomers did make amazing progress. The catch was that the pupils identified as 'academic bloomers' were chosen at random and that the progress these pupils made were attributed to their teachers' expectations. These pupils had lived up to their teachers' expectations. This study demonstrated what is now referred to as a self-fulfilling prophecy. Though this study is now very dated the impact of expectations are still very real and very powerful!

Further research states (Brophy and Good, 1970, Weinstein, 2004) that there are differences in how teachers treat pupils that they have *high expectations* for compared to pupils for which they hold *low expectations* and that these differences are evident in both verbal and non-verbal feedback. These differences are illustrated in Table 4.1. Of course, while aspiring to be a brilliant TA it is important to be aware of not only what you say but what your tone of voice and body language communicates.

The school has a key role to play in enabling each child to fulfil their learning potential. Maslow's (1908–1970) conceptualised ideas regarding optimal conditions for learning in his hierarchy of needs, the basic needs that must be met before psychological needs can be achieved. It is important to note that the top of the hierarchy – **self actualisation** is a goal which many continue to strive for throughout life (Figure 4.1).

Table 4.1 Actions that communicate low and high expectations

Actions that reflect low expectations	Actions that reflect high expectations
Less positive interactions, less eye contact, smiles less and less head nodding.	More positive interactions, more eye contact, smiles more, more head nodding.
Use more comfort talk. For example, 'not everyone can be good at maths.' Statements such as this encourages a fixed mindset.	Use less comfort talk. Encourage a can do attitude. Encouraging a growth mindset.
Asking fewer and less challenging questions, allowing little time for pupil to answer before providing the answer. Giving less informative feedback on answers.	Asking both more questions and more challenging questions. Waiting longer for pupils to answer them and spending more time elaborating or expanding on their answers.
Using less praise and offering praise for meeting minimal standards.	Using more praise but only offering praise for more rigorous and considered responses.

Source: Adapted from Fredricks, 2014, p. 216–217.

1. Self-actualisation

Schools can promote pupils' need for self-actualisation by encouraging pupils to fulfil their potential, recognise their strengths and challenging pupils to be the best they can be.

2. Esteem needs – feeling successful

Teachers/TAs can promote pupil self-esteem through: praise for effort as well as achievement and celebrating improvements in behaviour, learning and independence. Schools need to ensure that achievements are celebrated and acknowledged.

3. Social needs – love and belonging

Schools can be at the heart of communities. Schools can strive to be a place where all individuals perceive they are accepted, valued and belong. Simple strategies such as ensuring that you meet and greet everyone in a positive manner in addition to speaking to each child using positive affirmations ('It's good to see you at school today') will help children to feel valued.

4. Safety needs – feeling secure

Schools can support a pupil's need to feel safe through positive teacher/TA/pupil relationships, learning mentors and safeguarding procedures.

5. Physiological needs – nutrition, water, sleep, warmth

Schools can support physiological needs through school meals, information on healthy eating and living, ensuring pupils have access to drinking water and breakfast clubs. Schools can support parents through offering advice and support and can support pupils through the use of safeguarding procedures if neglect is suspected.

Figure 4.1 Maslow's hierarchy of needs and how schools can support these needs.

In summary, optimum conditions for learning would include:

- Having healthy relationships with encouraging adults who are sensitive to a child's need and respond accordingly;
- Having good role models;
- Comfortable and clean surroundings;
- A variety of experiences to draw on;
- Good levels of nutrition and sleep;
- Having high self-esteem and social and academic resilience;
- Having a sense of security and good mental wellbeing;
- Being curious, interested and able to appreciate and enjoy life.

Discussion point

Supporting pupils

Julia and Luke

Compare the two children described below in terms of their access to the optimum conditions for learning and Maslow's hierarchy of needs. What are their individual strengths and weaknesses? What can the school do to support these pupils?

Julia is in Year 6. She is a well-dressed child who has her own tablet, TV and mobile phone. She attends a gymnastics club as well as Scouts. SATs are approaching and she is under pressure from home to do well. Her parents work in professional roles and expect that Julia will get good grades. They rarely come to the school and have missed several Parent Consultation evenings. Julia is struggling as the demands of the curriculum become harder. Julia often loses her place in maths and English and is struggling to copy quickly enough from the board. Until this year learning has been quite easy for her. She is quiet and polite, always keen to please and well-behaved. Julia is not allowed to invite friends home. She often stays up late unnoticed using her tablet. Julia confides in her TA that she feels lonely and unhappy.

Luke is in Year 4. He has an Education, Health and Care Plan. He has cerebral palsy and is a wheelchair user. He has some involuntary movements and his speech is sometimes difficult to understand but developing well. He attends the local mainstream school and has a small group of friends with whom he interacts well. The school has made some adaptions for Luke and his wheelchair but this was well planned and his mum and dad have a good relationship with the school. Dad works away a lot, however the family are well supported by grandparents and Luke feels loved and an important part of his family. The family makes ends meet but do not have much left over for holidays and treats. Luke's TA is very aware of Luke's needs. Everyone encourages Luke's independence wherever possible. Luke is meeting age-related expectations in some areas and is slightly below in others.

As TAs you are closely involved with children's learning, often one to one or in small groups. You are able to observe and assess pupil's learning as well as having the opportunity to develop good relationships with pupils. As a TA you are also in a position to notice when learning difficulties occur, reflect on the reasons why and importantly communicate your concerns to the teacher. Through developing sensitive and empathetic relationships with the pupils you have the ability to influence the context and the conditions for learning.

Cognitive learning theories

Cognitive development is concerned with how children learn to process information which is taken in through the senses, including vision, hearing, sight, touch and taste. We process this information in order to evaluate, categorise, compare, sequence and generally make sense of our world. As we develop into mature adults we develop a range of higher order thinking skills which help us to negotiate day-to-day living. The crucial social and cognitive skill of understanding cause and effect is a higher order thinking skill necessary for every day negotiation of behaviour and relationships. To begin, hopefully a very young baby will learn that when they cry someone will come to 'lovingly tend' to their needs. As they mature they will learn both what is acceptable and unacceptable behaviour and that there are consequences for hitting their baby brother or talking in a disrespectful manner to their teacher. These higher order thinking skills, such as the awareness that actions have consequences, needs to be cultivated and encouraged in children. As we mature and become adults we become increasingly aware of how our behaviour may make someone else think or feel. We are able to reflect on the consequences of driving too fast or being impatient with children who we support when we are in a bad mood. This higher order thinking helps us not only to behave better but to develop moral reasoning.

In the past cognitive and behavioural psychologists used a combination of experimentation and observation to formulate their ideas about how we learn. They would construct and repeat experiments and observations to theorise about learning strategies. Famous examples such as the Swiss psychologist Piaget's Three Mountains test, which looks at how children take others perspective, have been replicated many times. Piaget's (1896–1980) work was widely disseminated in the 1960s and beyond. It led to 'child centred learning' which was highly influential in providing a more experiential, hands-on curriculum in nurseries and primary schools. Children were free to experiment with materials and resources at their own level just like those toddlers and children in the pool (Case Study 4.1) experimented with a range of water toys, poured water from buckets, tried to sieve it – all the while learning at their own pace and from their own motivation.

Constructivism

From Piaget's experiments and observations he concluded that children universally passed through set stages of thinking from early sensory and kinaesthetic learning through to later logical and abstract thinking. Piaget believed that children were 'lone scientists' who interacted with the world and actively constructed their own knowledge and ideas through 'schemas' which altered as experiences changed how children viewed the world. For example, toddlers may develop a schema concerning birds where initially all birds may be called 'ducks', but as their experience of birds grows beyond the visit to the ducks in the park, and they begin to compare and contrast other birds, their schema will expand to incorporate different types of birds with a variety of names (to include: swans, robins, blue jays, the albatross and blackbirds).

Piaget's belief that children actively construct their own knowledge, by experimenting and adapting their schema, led to the concept known as constructivism. This differed from the historical view that children were merely empty vessels to be filled with knowledge chosen by adults. Through questioning, toddlers and children are trying to make sense of the world and fit their newly acquired knowledge into new or existing schemas.

Vygotsky and the zone of proximal development (ZPD)

The views of the social constructivist Lev Vygotsky (1896–1934) and his concept of the zone of proximal development (ZPD) are still widely referred to in any discussion about learning. The ZPD is the distance between what a learner can do by themselves, that is, independently (the zone of actual development) and the level of potential development that could be reached with the support of an adult or *more knowledgeable other (MKO)*. Central to Vygotsky's views on learning is his belief that we learn best with the support of the more knowledgeable other (MKO), or, that we learn best within a 'social' context. This expert or MKO could be a parent, teacher, sibling or peer, who understands what you know now (zone of actual development) and can guide, or scaffold your learning forward to enable you to reach your potential in learning. Scaffolding refers to the temporary support provided by the more knowledgeable other (MKO) that enables the learner to complete the task. For children to progress in their learning there needs to be a MKO to help facilitate this process.

Vygotsky's views have influenced much of the organisation of learning in classrooms today. When planning a topic, effective teachers consider the 'prior knowledge' of their pupils at a class, group and individual level that is, their zone of actual development. Teachers consider how much support is needed in order for children to achieve their learning goals. Support could be in the form of adult and/or peer guidance or specific resources and equipment. Teachers may group their classes in mixed ability groups in order that higher achieving children can support lower achieving children. After a task has been completed teachers can then assess whether or not pupils have reached their goal and if not what further support can be given to help them. Vygotsky did not intend that adults simply tell the child how to solve problems or give them the answers but rather that they are guided and supported to do so creatively.

Skilled teachers will know their pupils well and assess the stage the children are at correctly. They will know the amount of challenge that is needed for each pupil. The task should be at the right level for the child to succeed without being too challenging.

Jerome Bruner (1915–2016) was a social constructivist and was inspired by the work of Vygotsky. Bruner is known for introducing the term 'scaffolding', where scaffolding is defined as the support offered to a child to learn a skill. Considering when to support and knowing when and how to withdraw support is key. An example of scaffolding is using arm bands with children learning to swim. As soon as they are not needed they are withdrawn. In more formal learning situations the amount of verbal support in terms of cues to solve a problem can also be viewed as scaffolding. Our aim is always to encourage independence and to withdraw support as soon as possible.

Bruner also believed that you could teach any subject to a child at a developmentally appropriate level and that children could later revisit the subject and add more complex skills or knowledge when ready. This is the basis of the 'spiral curriculum.' The national curriculum is based upon this principle.

The work of Piaget, Vygotsky and Bruner have influenced the way teaching has developed in many of countries although interpretations of their ideas have varied from country to country (Ileris, 2007).

A checklist for offering support

When you are asked to support individuals or groups of pupils it is important to be able to answer the following questions:

What do you want the pupils to be able to achieve?

This could be seen in relation to what you would like the pupils:

To do – What skills do they need to develop? (i.e., How to use a protractor.)

To know – What knowledge, content or understanding do they need to develop? (i.e., That there are 360 degrees are in a circle.)

To practice – What application or generalisation do they need to make? (i.e., Draw a range of angles accurately and compare them.)

What is their prior knowledge?

What do they already **know**? For example this could relate to vocabulary or concepts. In a maths lesson this could relate to their knowledge of concepts such as angle, degree or protractor. What can they already **do**? For example what skills have they already mastered? In a maths lesson this could relate to their knowledge of how to use a ruler to draw a straight line or to identify right angles.

In terms of this lesson plan

How will you extend their learning?
How much challenge is there in this task?
Is this task within their zone of proximal development?

Collaboration

Who will work best together and support each other?
What support will they need to achieve the task?
Who will give the support?

Assessment

How will you know when they have achieved the outcome? Do you need to record this? How will you record this?

Evaluation

Was the task too easy, too hard or at the right level?
Where will you take this activity next?
How will you feedback your thoughts to the teacher?

games. Older children copied the behaviours of even older children and children whose parents were actively teaching them to swim tried to copy what they had been shown.

Albert Bandura (b. 1925) in making links between behaviourist and cognitive psychology researched widely into the role of imitation or what he referred to as social learning. Bandura believed that children learn primarily through imitation, modelling and observing others. You can discover Bandura's famous 1961 Bobo Doll experiment online and see how the behaviour of children was affected by what they had recently observed. Bandura's theories still have relevance today when we discuss the impact of media violence (TV, film, computer games, etc.) on children.

Modelling is central to learning and is a means by which we can teach children. In classrooms this is known as the 'watch and learn' approach. However, modelling is not straightforward and involves a number of components or steps, these being:

1   Paying attention: In order to imitate a child must first pay attention to what is being demonstrated. However, the child may need to be advised as to what specific features of the activity they need to focus on.

2   Retention: To imitate or repeat a behaviour a child must remember the sequence of activities that make up the behaviour, that is they must store this knowledge and then be able to retrieve or recall this knowledge when needed. For example, as a TA you may first explain and demonstrate the steps for solving a maths problem to a pupil; then the next time you work with that pupil, you might say, 'Last time I showed you the steps – now can you try to do this yourself?' At this point the pupil needs to remember what to do but this very much depends on them having stored the information in the first place.

3   Motor reproduction processes: This involves both remembering what to do and involves the necessity of practising. For example a pupil may be shown by their TA how to write the Letter 'W.' The pupil has paid attention, the pupil has remembered but still the pupil will need to practice the sequence of movements in order to perfect their writing.

4   Motivational processes: Motivation is central to the ability to imitate. If a pupil is not motivated then it is unlikely they will pay attention in the first place. Even if a pupil has watched the behaviour, remembered the behaviour and has the ability to replicate the behaviour they may decide they do not want to.

Of course in a classroom, teachers and TAs act as models and often deliberately model or demonstrate behaviour that they wish pupils to learn, however other pupils can be powerful role models. Sometimes it is helpful to ask a pupil who is struggling to go and watch another pupil to see how they do it. Here a distinction is made between mastery and coping role models. A *mastery role model* is a person who is 'the expert', the person who can do the task with ease. However if there is too much of a difference between the pupil who needs to learn and the pupil who is the expert, then the pupil who is struggling may feel that the task is just too difficult for them and they may just give up. Here it is helpful to ask the pupil to watch and learn from a pupil who can act as a *coping role model*, that is, a pupil who is slightly more advanced and like them has experienced difficulties in learning and has made mistakes but has not given up.

Neuroscience

Nowadays we have the huge benefits of Magnetic Resonance Imaging (MRI) and Functional Magnetic Resonance Imaging (FMRI) scanning to actually see the brain in action as we perform tasks such as: memorising, predicting, categorising and sequencing and performing physical actions. We are at the early stages of this exciting science, and its application to schools is sometimes referred to as 'neuroeducation' or 'educational neuroscience.' There is a current debate about the usefulness of this research in education, however many teachers and educators are excited by the possibilities of brain research in influencing the way we teach.

We need to proceed with caution as some 'neuromyths' have been accepted as truths in the classroom without concrete evidence, for example categorising children as visual, auditory or kinaesthetic (VAK) learners (Goswami, 2015). For most children most of the time, the brain uses every part in all observed activities, that is, the auditory, visual and language areas are all *firing neurons* in every task. Learners may have a *preference* for work presented in a certain style but it is a limiting belief if children are taught that they can learn in only one particular way.

Learners can have preferences for how and where they learn, some like to study in silence, others prefer to have music playing. Some like the window open, some like to be warm. Some prefer to work with someone else, others are better on their own. Some pupils timetable frequent breaks with rewards, others plough on until they have finished. These are not learning styles but *preferences* for our learning environment.

It is the teaching rather than the learning that should be multi-sensory and creative, using a variety of ways to present information and make lessons interesting and fun.

Case study 4.4: How to teach using multi-sensory techniques

James is a bright boy who struggles to read and write. He has a diagnosis of dyslexia and Veronica, the class TA, supports James. Veronica practices phonics with James daily. Veronica has been trained to ensure that work for James is presented in a multi-sensory way. They trace and write the grapheme in cursive handwriting, they use sandpaper letters, and draw pictures that start with or include the sound. Veronica is helping James to understand that a certain letter or a number of letters (a grapheme) represents certain sound (phoneme). Veronica gets James to identify plastic letters from a feely bag, practice saying the sound *out loud*, and use a familiar picture as a cue for the phoneme (sound). Veronica helps James to create personally meaningful rhymes and definitions for words containing targeted sounds. Veronica begins to see that James is making progress with the multi-sensory approach to learning. In the multi-sensory approach each strategy reinforces the other. Repetition and practice is very important as it helps James build up strong neural pathways to remember the information taught.

Having seen success with James, Veronica tries to apply her understanding of this multi-sensory approach to teaching and supporting learning with other pupils in a variety of subjects. Explicitly thinking about different auditory, visual and kinaesthetic strategies has helped Veronica with the *on the spot* differentiation which her role often requires.

Neuroscience is shedding light upon conditions such as: ADHD, dyslexia and other brain based difficulties. Links between attention, emotion and social skills and how these areas affect learning and cognition are being explored. Further knowledge regarding sound processing and visual recognition may lead us to having improved systems for teaching reading. Despite much research neuroscientists would be the first to say that they are not in the business of providing quick fix solutions, though the hope is that research will lead to important and exciting discoveries which will inform classroom practice.

Meta-cognition

Meta-cognition is simply thinking about your own thinking and learning. Children should be taught explicitly to understand how to think, problem solve and be aware of strategies they can use. Meta-cognition can be viewed as having two strands; meta-cognitive knowledge and self-regulation.

Having meta-cognitive knowledge includes being aware of what skills or techniques aid learning. This may include: having an essay plan or a writing template to structure the work; a revision timetable; knowing the steps for solving a maths equation and being aware of what they find difficult and what they need to do when learning challenges occur. Knowing how you learn best, knowing which strategies to use to complete a task and being able to select the most appropriate strategy for the task are all forms of meta-cognitive awareness.

Being able to self-regulate, when applied to learning, involves the ability to:

- direct your attention effectively;
- plan how to approach a task;
- monitor your progress in carrying out the task;
- evaluating how successful you have been and;
- learning how to improve your ability to learn.

Assessment for learning strategies are one way in which schools try to promote meta-cognition giving clear objectives for learning and realistic feedback for improvement. Further pupils need to know the success criteria, that is, both the learning intentions of the task and what they need to do to achieve success. The language that teachers and TAs use when discussing work with children is crucial to pupil development of meta-cognitive awareness. Elaborating and extending children's thinking through constructive and targeted feedback to both pupil written work and their spoken contributions in class is an important skill to learn. Being able to extend pupils' knowledge, is a skill to be practised and refined. We will discuss this further in Chapter 7.

teacher. The class teacher arranges a meeting with Anna's mum and the Special Educational Needs Coordinator (SENCo). The SENCo says that it could be a working memory problem and gives mum, Anna and the teacher some practical ideas to try with Jacob.

These strategies include the following:

Anna teaching Jacob to use a note book to draw or note instructions.
Encouraging the use of memory aids for example, wall charts, flash cards, writing frames that Jacob can refer to.
Encouraging Jacob to ask for repetition of instructions.
Have the teacher train a friend of Jacob's to be his memory buddy. If Jacob is struggling to remember what he needs to do, he now has a designated person, his memory buddy, to go to for assistance.

These small differences start to have an effect on Jacob's self-esteem. When his memory difficulties are discussed with him he realises that he can do things to help himself. He knows that he can learn and understand if he uses strategies and receives support. Jacob's mum now understands why he struggles to do what she asks and there are less arguments at home. Anna now knows indicators of working memory difficulties and what to look out for with the other pupils she supports. See Table 4.2.

Table 4.2 How the school day may be difficult if you have a poor working memory

Examples of activities	Difficulty	Support
Remembering the instructions for sports day given in Assembly.	Too much to process and remember.	Use a memory buddy. Use a visual timetable.
Learning vocabulary for parts of a plant for science.	Too many unfamiliar words at once. Cannot learn the word and the function or meaning easily.	Pre-teach the words using a variety of strategies (multi-sensory approach).
Playing football in the playground.	Difficulty remembering who is on which team and the direction of play.	Give coloured armbands. Use a memory buddy.
Mental maths timed test.	Unable to keep the numbers in mind and process them.	Allow a whiteboard to write on or provide written numbers. Not a realistic activity for pupils with a poor working memory.

Attachment

We have seen the importance of learning in a social environment – from Vygotsky's more knowledgeable other (MKO), Bruner's scaffolding, using rewards, encouraging imitation and modelling and giving feedback. These are all socially mediated strategies for learning. These strategies are effective because the human baby is the most socially influenced creature on earth (Gerhardt, 2004). We reach independence later in human society than any other animal. However crucial patterns for learning and emotional responses affecting our motivation and learning are embedded in that first special relationship with our primary caregiver, usually but not always, the mother. Important foundations for early learning are laid down in the first years of life in our relationship with our primary caregiver.

John Bowlby (1907–1990) is known as the father of attachment theory. He studied bonding and attachment in humans. Bowlby believed that this first attachment is different from any other attachment and that breakdown in this relationship can lead to behavioural and mental health problems in later life. Bowlby defined the nature of the mother/caregiver baby relationship as a two-way reciprocal relationship, based on attuning and regulating the baby's emotions. *Attunement* is the careful reading and appropriate and supportive response to another's emotional state. Babies whose emotions are well-regulated by happy and attuned parents will thrive. The developing child will learn to regulate their own emotions if they are soothed when crying or distressed. Babies whose caregivers are depressed, or have few support networks, may do less well in developing the secure relationships that provide young children with the optimum conditions for learning (Gerhardt, 2004).

Bowlby's findings were taken a step further by Mary Ainsworth (1973) who identified different types of attachment styles, and more recently by the work of Heather Geddes (2005) who wrote, 'Attachment in the classroom: the links between children's early experience, emotional wellbeing and performance in school.' See Table 4.3.

On your journey to become a brilliant TA you may encounter children whose behaviour can be frustrating and challenging. Take time to consider how they relate to the adults around them.

Remember all is not lost if a child's early attachments are less than perfect as later positive affirming relationships with adults can heal earlier difficult relationships; this is where caring and empathetic TAs can make a real difference! All adults who come into contact with children who have experienced difficulties in attachment can have an

Table 4.3 Attachment styles and how they may appear in the classroom

Attachment Styles		Emotional state of child	What this attachment style may look like in the classroom (Geddes, 2005)	Some suggested ways forward (Geddes, 2005)
Attachment	Experience			
Secure	Responsive caregiver regulates the baby's emotions.	Contented, explorative child who trusts their needs will be met.	Here the pupil is confidently able to work on tasks, to include challenging tasks and to accept help from the teacher.	Child will benefit from all learning strategies and support.
Avoidant	Emotionally unavailable, distant, disengaged caregiver.	A child that does not expect needs to be met. Child can become distant and unemotional. Child could be seen as independent.	While the pupil is content and feels safe to work on given tasks the pupil finds it difficult or uncomfortable to engage with the teacher/TA. This pupil will find it difficult to ask for help and feels a need to be independent from the teacher/TA.	The presence of another child can help the child cope with the presence of an adult. Giving very clear instructions can help the child feel that they know what they should be doing.
Resistant/ Ambivalent Attachment	Care given is inconsistent, changes from sensitive to neglectful.	Child can be confused, perhaps clingy. Child not able to rely on needs being met. May be angry and anxious.	The pupil may appear anxious and uncertain. Here the pupil does relate to adults in the room but may seem to be over-dependent or clingy.	Reliable consistent adult support is advised. To reduce anxiety and uncertainty, provide pupil with information on beginnings, separations, endings, changes, class movements and disruptions in routine.

Disorganised	Care given is very erratic - can be frightening to the child. Care can be either passive or overly intrusive at different times. Child experiences extremes of behaviour from caregiver.	Child can be extremely confused, very anxious and hyper-vigilant. May feel that there is no way of getting needs met.	Pupil may be extremely anxious though the pupil will deal with these feelings by needing to be in control at all times. The fear of not knowing is so difficult that it can trigger feelings of incompetence, humiliation and rejection. The pupil may be unable to accept being taught and that others know more than they do.	This pupil will need a school environment that is safe, reliable and predictable.

effect on helping them to change their reactions and become more confident and secure.

The awareness of the effect of poor attachments on children's learning is now much greater in schools with many schools becoming 'Attachment Friendly.' Training is available for all staff to recognise and work with pupils using a variety of strategies often delivered by educational psychologists. Strategies such as: meet and greet by a key worker and support from an Emotional Literacy Support Assistant are now helping children achieve their potential.

Language development

Language development is closely connected to attachment in that the reciprocal relationship between mother (primary caregiver) and baby forms the earliest phase of language development. The response to early babbling and gestures, encouragement to speak and communicate is essential for healthy language development. The first two years of the caregiver/child relationship are crucial in that the communication background of a child, how they are listened to and talked and read with is a more important predictor of readiness for school than their parents' socioeconomic status (Goldin-Meadow et al., 2014). Children who have a rich home language experience start school with an advantage. Children from these 'language rich and privileged' families by the age of four have heard 30 million more words than children described as coming from less language enriched households (Hart and Risley, 1995). Indeed vocabulary size at age 5 is a very strong predictor of the qualifications achieved at school-leaving age and beyond (Feinstein and Duckworth, 2006). Gross (2013, p. 4) argues that language skills are a critical factor in social disadvantage and states that:

> On average a toddler from a family on welfare will hear around 600 words per hour, with a ratio of two prohibitions ('stop that', 'get down off there') to one encouraging comment. A child from a professional family will hear over 2000 words per hour, with a ratio of six encouraging comments to one negative.
>
> (Hart and Risley, 2003)

In looking forward, Hammer (2012) argues that by supporting parents to develop their children's language we could improve educational and life chances for many. Certainly schools will focus on providing an enriched language environment for all pupils. Central to providing an enriched language environment is asking questions and dialogic teaching which we will discuss further in Chapter 7.

Summary

On your journey to becoming a brilliant TA remember:

- Having high expectations of pupils are important;
- There are optimum conditions in which learning can occur;
- The learning of individual children can be affected by many inter-related social, emotional and cognitive factors;
- Positive early home learning experiences and attachment are crucial for promoting good mental health and cognitive skills, especially language development;
- The plasticity of the brain means that schools can use strategies to help compensate for missed early learning opportunities for some pupils;
- Learning is a social activity; parents, siblings, peers, teachers and TAs are all significant in the learning process.

Chapter 5

Understanding behaviour

Introduction

Behaviour is important! A pupil who listens, who participates, who is enthusiastic and who wants to learn is a joy to teach. Hopefully you work with such pupils but the question is: How do pupils cultivate these positive attributes for learning and what can you as a TA do to enable the pupils you work with to develop these skills?

But what is behaviour like in schools today? Recent media comments and headlines proclaim:

- 'Behaviour is a national problem in schools in England, a recent review finds' (*The Guardian*, March 24, 2017).
- 'Hundreds of knives sieved in 18 months at UK Schools figures show ... the majority of seizures involved children, including some as young as five' (Grierson, 2017).
- 'Ofsted inspectors were pelted with food in a classroom on a nightmare school visit' (*Telegraph*, 12 May, 2017).
- 'Unison survey of nearly 15,000 support staff reveals that of 53% of TAs surveyed said that they had experienced physical violence with 76% stating that they had witnessed violence at their schools in the past 12 months' (Unison, 2016).

However, challenging behaviour in schools is not new with research and policy documents noting that educators have identified challenging behaviour as a concern for schools for over forty years. Indeed delving into historical records reveals that this concern with young people extends far into the distant past; a 6,000-year-old Egyptian tomb had an inscription which bemoaned the fact that young people no longer respect their parents and are rude and impatient (Byron, 2009).

After reading these facts a number of questions come to mind?

- What is challenging behaviour?
- What are effective strategies for dealing with challenging behaviour?
- How do you promote positive attributes for learning?

Answering these questions will be the focus of this chapter.

What is challenging behaviour?

Tom Bennett in a recent report entitled, 'Creating a culture: How school leaders can optimise behaviour', defines behaviour as,

> Any actions performed by any members of the student and staff communities. It includes conduct in the classrooms and all public areas; how members work, communicate, relax and interact: how they study; how they greet staff; how they arrive at school, transition from one activity to another; how they use social media, and many other areas of their conduct. It does not merely refer to how students do or do not act antisocially.
>
> (Bennett, 2017, p. 12)

This is a key definition as it acknowledges the importance of not only the behaviour of the individual pupil but the collective behaviour of the entire school community.

When researching aspects of classroom behaviour there are a number of terms used to describe individual behaviour by a pupil that is not seen as optimal, these include phrases such as: challenging, disruptive, non-compliant and difficult, to name just a few. And of course your school will have its own terminology. The key point is that in using the terminology we must be careful that we are not creating a self-fulfilling prophecy, in that children and young people identify with the label (disruptive, difficult, challenging) and act accordingly. Tanya Byron (2009) notes that, 'children first become negatively labelled in nurseries and schools and often these labels stick'; to avoid this, educational professionals need to seek the reasons for pupil behaviour. One school of psychology, Behaviourism, argues that if a child or young person continues to behave in a certain way then that behaviour serves an important function for them; from *the pupil's* point of view the behaviour is rewarding or perhaps it allows them to escape from what they perceive to be an awful situation. The key point is that behaviour is always a form of communication!

At this point it is helpful to look at the following case studies.

Case study 5.1: 'Being Sam'

Sam does not like maths. Sam finds reading difficult and most of the time can't make sense of the textbooks or worksheets. However, Sam is proud and does not like to feel that he can't do things that all his other classmates seem to do easily. Sam does not like to ask for help and feels his teacher does not understand.

Mr Telford, the maths teacher, finds Sam difficult to work with. Sam just does not pay attention and Sam continually distracts other students and can be very rude, which is just not acceptable.

Sam realises that he says things he shouldn't but when he does – this results in him being sent to the behaviour unit where he is given a drink and biscuit to calm down. Sam prefers being in the unit where they seem to understand his difficulties.

Sam's behaviour is seen as challenging by his teacher; however, for Sam his behaviour serves an important function. Sam knows if he swears at his teacher he will be removed from a situation where he feels a failure and that he will be sent to a place where he feels safe.

Case study 5.2: 'Being Sally'

One day Lauren, a TA in a Year 7 English class, noticed Sally talking in a very loud manner to a fellow pupil (Jessica) on the other side of the room. Before Lauren or the teacher could react Sally picked up her textbook and threw it at Jessica. The teacher immediately told Sally that this was not acceptable and asked Lauren to take Sally to the behaviour unit. On the way to the unit, Sally, between sobs explained that her Dad had just left her Mom and that Jessica was teasing her at break and saying some nasty things about her mom.

Throwing a textbook at another pupil has never been acceptable and never will be. And yet behaviour is complex and Sally's behaviour though not condoned can be understood in view of the very difficult family situation she was facing. Rightly Lauren feeds this information back to the teacher and the teacher replies, 'Thank you for telling me why Sally was upset and I will talk to both Sally and Jessica about this.'

There are a number of points that these case studies raise:

- How we act is connected to how we feel and think;
- For some children and young people, behaviour is a way of communicating or an expression of 'what can't be said,' or 'is too painful to put into words';
- Emotional stability is necessary in order to learn. Children who can regulate their emotions or deal with difficult emotions in a positive manner are able to focus on what is required, follow instructions and learn;
- Knowing the reasons for behaviour can suggest strategies for turning the behaviour around; this would require helping the pupils in the examples, illustrated in Case Studies 5.1 and 5.2, to find ways of dealing constructively with difficult feelings, thoughts and emotions.

While aspiring to be a brilliant TA you are aiming to enable all pupils to achieve their potential. However, in order to learn pupils first need to develop certain attributes or behaviours for learning. As pupils have varying abilities and needs, so do they vary in terms of their readiness to engage in learning. Before we discuss how to create a classroom conducive to learning it is important to consider these individual attributes necessary for learning.

Table 5.1 is useful as it identifies characteristics that both lead to behaviour for learning and to pupils not achieving their potential, or having behaviours that we may see as challenging.

Table 5.1 Attributes for learning – Key terms

Student characteristic	What a student would say if they had this characteristic
Self-efficacy Refers to the belief in one's own competence or ability.	A pupil with a high level of self-efficacy when given a challenging task would say: 'I believe I can do this.'
Intrinsic/extrinsic motivation The degree to which personal motivation is controlled by internal (intrinsic) or external (extrinsic) factors.	The type of motivation a pupil has will influence the way they approach a task. If a pupil has intrinsic motivation then they might say: 'I am doing this because I enjoy it. Being able to participate in this task is all the reward I need.' On the other hand pupils who are extrinsically motivated are more likely to say, 'what's in it for me?' These students are driven by rewards, stars, stickers, merits and other valued consumables.
Self-handicapping behaviour When presented with an activity that a pupil believes they *can't* do, the pupil in order to maintain self-worth and self-esteem deliberately engages in self-sabotage to give themselves a plausible reason for failure.	Fearing that she will fail the upcoming test Jodie decides not to revise; therefore Jodie will be able to say to herself: 'I failed because I did not study'.
Mastery goal orientation The pupil sees the focus of learning as the opportunity to acquire additional knowledge or master new skills. Mastery goal orientation is often contrasted with performance goal orientation in which the pupil's desire is to demonstrate their superior ability to others in order to make a good impression. Students with a mastery goal orientation would also have intrinsic motivation and a growth mindset.	A student with a mastery goal orientation would say: 'I am doing this task because I want to learn and understand everything there is to know about this topic.'

Mindsets

Fixed and growth mindsets relate to beliefs that individuals have about how their intelligence develops. These beliefs have a profound impact on attitudes towards learning and achievement.

Pupils with a growth mindset would believe that working harder makes you smarter; that effort increases ability and that mistakes are opportunities to learn. A mistake is a signal to try a different strategy or approach.

Pupils with a fixed mindset would believe that if you have the ability then you don't need to work as knowledge would just come and that if you have to work then this would mean that you were not clever in the first place. Mistakes are seen as a reflection of lack of ability and a signal to give up.

Expectancy-value theory

This theory of motivation believes that in order to learn pupils must have both an expectation that they will succeed and value the task that is given to them. If a pupil values the task then they will find it interesting and see it as useful or relevant to future goals.

A pupil who has a passion for maths would obviously value input on maths. However a pupil who does not initially share this passion will need to be persuaded that maths is interesting, useful and relevant.

For example, a pupil might say: 'I thought that what we were doing in maths was useless until my TA explained that if I wanted to become a chef, then I would need these skills.'

Learned helplessness

A condition where a pupil perceives that they are powerless and that nothing they do will make any difference.

A pupil in Year 10, on the brink of being excluded, states: "What's the point in trying – even if I did something – it would not make a difference."

Self-regulation

Self-regulation involves the ability to think before you act and to act in your long-term best interest. Emotional self-regulation involves: the ability to deal with difficult emotions and feelings; the ability to calm yourself when you're upset or angry and cheer yourself up when you're feeling down or discouraged.

A pupil who is prone to angry outbursts but has attended sessions on emotional regulation, states:

'I have been taught to recognise when I am about to lose my temper and then I need to breathe in deeply and count to 10. If I am still feeling angry and I feel I need some time out then I am to show my red card to the teacher or TA.'

(Continued)

Table 5.1 Continued

Student characteristic	What a student would say if they had this characteristic
Deep/surface learning These terms apply to the depth of study or learning the pupil engages in and this depth of learning can best be seen along a spectrum. At one end you have deep learning which implies learning with the purpose of understanding and achieving mastery in the subject. At the other end of the spectrum, as the name implies, is surface learning; a student is going through the motions but not really retaining any information.	The TA asked, her group, 'How much do you remember from the work you did the previous year?' Most of the pupils reply: 'Well, I remember studying for the test, I read over all my notes but honestly I can't remember anything we did.' This is an example of surface learning. Another pupil comments, 'I spent a lot of time revising. I did read my notes but I also spent a lot of time trying to make sense of what I read and to connect it to others things that I already knew'. This is an example of deep learning.

Activity 5.1 Identifying characteristics needed for learning

For each of the following identify both characteristics you believe the pupil has and lacks. Use the key terms mentioned in Table 5.1. Also consider the strategies you would use to help the pupil develop positive attributes to learning.

Situation	Characteristics the pupil has	Characteristics they need to develop	Strategies you would use to help the student develop positive attributes to learning
Joe is faced with a maths test. Joe feels he is just not capable of doing this. Joe knows that one of his teeth is slightly wobbly and is soon to come out. Though it hurts, Joe pulls on his tooth till there is blood all over his test paper. Consequently Joe is removed from the room.			
Sam when faced with a problem he sees as difficult feels like a loser! Usually at this point he starts swearing at the teacher and is removed from the classroom.			

Depending on a pupil's readiness to learn they will behave very differently in the classroom. Fredricks (2014) argued that in any class pupils could be classified into those who are: fully engaged, behaviourally engaged only and at risk.

When looking at Table 5.2, think of the pupils you support – how would you classify them? When I have asked teachers and TAs to do this they are always able to identify some who are fully engaged and some who are at risk, but the majority of pupils they support they see, or label as, behaviourally engaged only. Is this your experience?

Table 5.2 Levels of engagement

Fully engaged, these pupils:	Behaviourally engaged only, these pupils:	At risk, these pupils:
• Are intrinsically motivated • Have self-regulation • Engage in deep learning • Have a growth mindset • Have good relationships with teachers and peers	• Participate • Are compliant – they only do just enough • Have a fixed mindset • Are anxious about challenges • Engage in surface learning	• Do not participate • Have poor relationships with teachers/peers • Display learned helplessness • Display avoidance tactics • Engage in self-handicapping behaviour • Lack parental support

Source: Adapted from Fredricks, 2014.

To be a brilliant TA you will need to have strategies to work with all pupils. The pupils who are fully engaged will still need encouragement and praise and could act as role models for the other pupils in the class.

The pupils in the 'behaviourally engaged only' group need support if they are to fulfil their learning potential. These pupils need strategies to develop growth mindsets, to overcome a fear of failure and to learn specific study skills necessary to engage in deep learning.

However, it may be that most of your time will be spent dealing with pupils who are deemed to be at risk.

There has been much written recently on mental health and mental wellbeing. Within the literature mental health disorders include: impulse control disorders; substance use disorders; anxiety and mood disorders and schizophrenia. Recent research (Knapp et al., 2016) reports that in an average class of thirty 15-year-old pupils:

- Three could have a mental disorder;
- Ten are likely to have witnessed their parents separate;
- One could have experienced the death of a parent;
- Seven are likely to have been bullied;
- Nine girls and three boys may be self-harming.

Added to these statistics is the prevalence of mental health problems higher in some groups, with 36 per cent of children and young people with a learning disability also having mental health problems (Emerson and Hatton, 2007); and approximately 60 per cent of children and young people in care being diagnosed with a mental disorder (NICE, 2012).

Within the field of mental health many practitioners make reference to a classic study conducted in the 1990s by Vincent Felitti and Robert Anda (Centers for Disease Control and Prevention) (Felitti et al., 1998). The focus of their study was on Adverse Childhood Experiences (ACEs) which included experiences such as: maltreatment, neglect, abuse, having a family member in prison, growing up in care and living in a household where someone abuses alcohol or drugs. This study established a link between ACEs and the impact on emotional and physical health in later life. Simply Felitti and Anda (Anda et al., 2010) argued that what happens in childhood matters!

I have mentioned some very alarming statistics regarding mental health. But what can a teacher or TA do? Teachers and TAs need to be on the watch for early indicators or warning signs. These warning signs include: loneliness, low levels of self-worth, difficulties in friendships, difficulties in family relationships, bullying, reports of being depressed, reports of self-harming, feelings of not belonging and low levels of self-confidence. Of course, if you do see something of concern then you must report this. In the first place always talk to your teacher (see information on safeguarding p. 48).

Recognising that mental health is everyone's concern, there are initiatives that aim to improve mental health and wellbeing in schools. These initiatives are important as increases in pupil mental health and wellbeing will lead to better pupil attainment, attendance and behaviour and more favourable outcomes for children and young people in adulthood. A proactive approach is needed where a greater emphasis is placed on prevention and early intervention. As the quote says: "It is easier to build strong children than to repair broken men" (Frederick Douglass, 1818–1895).

Examples of whole school initiatives would include approaches to promoting resilience, growth mindsets, supporting social and emotional learning and teaching strategies for emotional regulation (see Chapter 8 for examples). It may seem like common sense, but kind words are important and empathetic teachers and TAs can help pupils achieve their potential. However, ultimately the goal for teachers and TAs is to help children and young people develop their own strategies to enable them to deal with life in a positive and constructive manner.

What are the most effective strategies for dealing with challenging behaviour?

Creating a culture

Tom Bennett in his review of behaviour in schools (2017, p. 6) argues that a transformation in school culture is needed in order to optimise behaviour.

The key task for a school leader is to create a culture – usefully defined as 'the way we do things around here' that is understood and subscribed to by the whole school community.

(Bennett, 2017, p. 6)

Further Bennett (2017) argues that this approach needs: visible leaders, detailed expectations, high staff support, an ethos that all students matter, attention to detail, staff engagement and consistent practices.

This theme of creating a culture is further described by Ron Berger (2003) where he argues that 'the attitudes and achievements of students are shaped by the culture around them: Students adjust their attitudes and efforts in order to fit into the culture' (Berger, 2003, p. 34).

Therefore the culture that is created in the school, the classroom and moment-by-moment in specific lessons is crucial. A culture for excellence, according to Berger (2003) implies that all pupils have internalised the value of striving to be the best that they can be. However, it is easy to see how a peer culture that ridicules academic effort and achievement can develop through pupils believing that it is not cool to raise your hand in class or to do homework. Here it is important to reflect on how as a brilliant TA do you help pupils 'to want' to achieve their potential?

To create a culture of excellence constructive feedback is crucial. Often in schools pupils will be given a piece of work, complete the work, be given feedback on the set work only to move onto the next task. According to Berger (2012) one way forward, in the process of creating a culture of excellence, is for pupils to work on projects where multiple drafts are required. Within this process the pupil attempts the task and receives initial feedback in that, 'yes that was good but it could be even better if.' The pupil then reworks their project to submit it for further constructive comments and this process repeats itself several times. The result of this drafting process is that the end product is a work that the pupil can be truly proud of and often the work produced is so much more than the pupil ever thought possible. A brilliant example of this can be found on the YouTube clip, entitled: 'Austin's Butterfly' (Berger, 2012). Teachers and TAs are key to establishing a culture that optimises behaviour and as stated before this culture is created on a whole school level, within the classroom and moment-by-moment within each lesson.

One further important way to achieve this culture for success is to follow school policies and procedures relating to behaviour, sanctions and rewards. To be a brilliant TA you will need to be able to work within these systems.

Activity 5.2 How do you work within systems and procedures?

At the university where we work and as part of our research for this book we asked the TAs on our Foundation degree what sanctions and rewards they could administer. What follows is their replies. How would you respond to these questions?

Sanctions	Sanctions I can give on my own initiative	Though I can give this sanction on my own initiative, I always make a point of informing the teacher of what I have done	I can give this sanction but only after first consulting the teacher	These sanctions are to be used only by the teacher or a member of the Senior Management Team (SMT)	Not relevant in my school
Reminder of classroom rules I can ...	88%	12%			
Names recorded for misbehaviour – if there are two entries, a pupil will miss their break I can ...	34%	39%	5%		22%
Handing out warning cards I can ...	41%	24%			35%
Giving extra work I can ...	12%	35%	23%	6%	24%
Moving pupil to another desk I can ...	44%	33%	12%	5%	6%
Asking pupil to wait outside the room as a time-out measure	35%	18%	12%	6%	29%

I can ...	Rewards I can give on my own initiative	Though I can give this reward on my own initiative, I always make a point of informing the teacher of what I have done	I can give this reward but only after first consulting the teacher	These rewards are to be used only by the teacher or a member of the SMT	Not relevant in my school
Removing pupil from class	35%	12%	6%	29%	18%
Giving a 10 minute detention	18%	18%	5%	18%	41%
Giving a longer detention with a teacher	6%	6%	6%	23%	59%
Arranging for parents to come in to discuss issues of concern	6%	12%	18%	59%	5%

Rewards	Rewards I can give on my own initiative	Though I can give this reward on my own initiative, I always make a point of informing the teacher of what I have done	I can give this reward but only after first consulting the teacher	These rewards are to be used only by the teacher or a member of the SMT	Not relevant in my school
Praise	100%				
Hand out stickers	100%				
Hand out merit points	82%	6%			12%
Fill in home/school book informing parents/carers of good behaviour	65%	18%			17%
Contact parents/carers about good behaviour	35%	18%	6%	35%	6%

I am sure you found it interesting to compare the responsibilities you have with others. When we received the results from the Behaviour questionnaire in Activity 5.2 from the TAs we work with, what we noted is how much TA roles and responsibilities vary from school to school! And of course TAs who work with a number of teachers will know that often teachers have their own expectations.

Emma Clarke and John Visser (2017, p. 74) conducted interviews and focus groups with TAs and found that though TAs acknowledged:

> how important it was to know children to effectively manage their behaviour however, lack of consistency in teacher's expectations and TA deployment made this challenging and therefore managing behaviour harder. The lack of clarity over teacher expectations and TA role definition placed further tension on TAs' desire to 'help and support' teachers without undermining them.

Therefore – the key point for an aspiring brilliant TA is *'How do I come to an understanding of what I can do and what are the limits to my authority?'*

Case study 5.3: Just a story

The setting is a secondary school. It is a Monday morning and a teacher is encouraging his Year 9 students to enter the classroom in an orderly manner and settle down to work. In the class there is a TA.

The teacher tries to settle the class and explain the lesson objectives. The class proves difficult to settle. There is some playful fighting, constant chatter and the teacher fails to make himself heard above the din. The teacher tries again and again to settle the class. The TA tries to assist the teacher by reminding individual pupils to behave, but the class do not settle. The TA spends the lesson working with a small group of pupils.

The lesson continues in that the teacher tries and tries to gain control but to no avail. The lesson objectives are assigned as homework. Later at break, the TA discusses the lesson with the Higher Level Teaching Assistant (HLTA).

The TA asks the HLTA what she should do.

TA: Can I take control of the class? Can I yell at them? Can I tell the pupils to be quiet and listen and to show the teacher some respect? What would he think if I did this?

> HLTA: No you can't. Perhaps, as you say, the lesson was not per-
> ceived as engaging or relevant and it was too quick in pace;
> however, at best you can suggest a change in the seating plan
> to the teacher.
>
> The HLTA later discusses the situation with theSpecial Education Needs
> Coordination (SENCo).
>
> SENCo: Yes that is a difficult situation. According to our behaviour pol-
> icy any member of staff deals with poor behaviour when they
> see it within the guidelines of our behaviour policy. However
> TAs are right to be worried about stepping on toes. Some
> teachers are very happy for TAs to step in and give official
> warnings and likewise some teachers are not. Mrs Jay in the
> Nurture group insists that she addresses all behaviour issues
> herself. I see it as my role to be the Middle Man, so to speak,
> when TAs have issues with teachers. I will talk to the teacher.
> Perhaps his lesson was not engaging and perhaps the pace was
> too quick but even as a fellow teacher I would need to be very
> thoughtful regarding how I have that conversation.

Though Case Study 5.3 is just a story it does reflect tensions regarding roles and responsibilities between teachers and teaching assistants and as such variations on the above story occur on a daily basis across the country. But what is the way forward? Perhaps as an aspiring brilliant TA there is a need to be proactive. Talk to the teacher at the beginning of the year to clarify their expectations, 'What can you do?', 'What can't you do?' and when there are episodes of challenging behaviour what would the teacher you support like you to do? Remember it is always important to be singing from the same song sheet (see p. 124 for information on teacher/TA contracts).

How do you promote positive attributes for learning?

Praise be

Praise is incredibly powerful! To give praise is to communicate that 'I like you' and people who feel they are liked are often more likely to behave positively than people who feel disliked. So as a TA the ability to give praise is an important part of your toolkit. Yet praise is complex!

Some TAs tell cautionary tales of how they commented on how wonderful a piece of work was only for the pupil to burst into tears, rip up the work and storm out of the room. Other TAs tell stories of how even young children seem to become so addicted to praise, merit points and rewards that they have become so to speak, 'sticker junkies.' So what is this all about? Again, the act of giving praise is complex. Do you recall the saying: 'beauty is in the eye of the beholder?' Well praise is like that. For praise to work, that is, to make a child feel good and want to repeat the behaviour the child must perceive what is said as a praise statement.

Perception is everything. From a pupils' perspective it is not just what you say but how they make sense of what you say. Your tone of voice and body language communicate important messages. In addition the child or young person's beliefs and feelings about themselves act as a filter in terms of how they interpret the message.

Looking at research is helpful at this point. The cognitive evaluation theory (Deci and Moller, 2005) states that rewards have the potential to both **control** and **inform**, and it is how the pupil interprets the 'praise message' that is crucial.

Case study 5.4: The praise message

Imagine you are in an English class and a child has written an amazing piece of work.

Rightly you state: 'That was an absolutely amazing piece of work, your use of adjectives is really improving. I am going to recommend that you receive a merit point for this work!'

Now imagine that the pupil continues to do great work and you as the TA continue to praise them.

However, after a while the pupil starts to think and reflect about why they are spending time and effort writing. At this point there are two possible interpretations.

Version 1: The pupil could say:

I am putting in all this time and effort writing stories when I could be going out with my mates. Yet I love writing stories. I like the praise I get in terms of comments from the teacher and TA and I like getting top grades and merit points and the comments are helpful in telling me how I could improve. But even if I didn't get the top grades or merit points or praise it would not really make a difference – I just love writing and writing is part of who I am.

In this example, the pupil perceives that praise is used to *inform* him of what to do next – that is how to improve. This pupil, in this example, is intrinsically motivated to write.

Version 2: Alternatively the pupil could state:

I am putting in all this time and effort writing stories when I could be going out with my mates. Ok, I like the praise I get in terms of comments from the teacher and TA and I like getting merit points. But I feel I am being rewarded like I reward my dog for sitting up. Merit points are for kids.

In this example, the pupil perceives that the praise and merit points are *controlling* his behaviour of writing and therefore he decides to no longer put in the time and effort to write.

From the perspective of the teacher and the TA this is a sad outcome, as the pupil showed great promise.

Case Study 5.4 powerfully illustrates that it is not what you say *but how what you say is interpreted.* So what can teachers and TAs do? Though praise is important it is also important to help pupils see the relevance of the activity for themselves, that is, to encourage intrinsic motivation. But how do you know what is the right way to praise a pupil? Here I am reminded of a teacher who on the first day of school every year would praise each pupil, in turn, as they entered the classroom. For example she might say: 'I liked the way you entered the classroom' or 'I liked the way you helped your fellow student.' The clever bit was that as the teacher was praising them she was also analysing and making notes of how each of her pupils responded to praise. Some of the pupils she noted lapped up praise while other pupils seemed distinctly uncomfortable with the attention. This information was important in that it helped her decide how best to relate to each individual child within her classroom. From her experience every pupil had his or her own unique praise style.

One way to ascertain a pupil's praise style is to ask for their perceptions; here Activity 5.3 can be very useful.

Activity 5.3 How to determine a pupil's unique praise style?

Ask the pupils you support the following:

Think about all the times you do something well, it doesn't matter which subject or work you are thinking of. Think about the good behaviour and choices you make.

When you do something well, what does your teacher/TA usually say to you?

And what would you like them to say or do if you do something well?

Comments from Activity 5.3 can be very revealing. What you hope to find is a match between what you actually, 'say or do' and what the pupil prefers in terms of praise.

So ideally the pupil would say:	When I have done something well or tried hard, my teacher or TA they move me up a place on the chart and say, 'Well Done'. I like it the way it is. I don't want it to change.
However, imagine the following:	
A pupil states:	No one notices what I do. Everyone is praised more than me ... I feel invisible.

This last reply is worrying. However, it may be that from the teacher's and TA's perspective they are praising the student. In fact they may believe they are praising the pupil all the time! *The important point of this example is that perception is all! At this point what is needed is a very sensitive discussion with the pupil in regards to what the pupil sees as praise and what praise they would like.*

Creating the conditions in which pupils will motivate themselves

As an aspiring to be brilliant TA, one proactive means of promoting behaviour for learning is to find ways of motivating the pupils you support. As Deci (2012) argued it is important to ask not only how you can motivate others but how you can create the conditions in which the pupils you support will motivate themselves.

Ryan and Deci (2002, 2008) argued, in their self-determination theory, that humans have three basic needs: the need for competence, autonomy and relatedness. Within this theory these needs are defined as:

Competence: The need to be effective in dealing with the environment; the need to feel you are functioning successfully and that you are managing life's demands.

Autonomy: The need to feel in control over what happens on a day-by-day level; the ability to have choices.

Relatedness: The need to have positive relationships with others.

Therefore, the pupils you support in order to achieve their learning potential will need to feel that they are competent, that they have autonomy and that they have a sense of relatedness, that is, they need to experience a sense of belonging, of being liked and valued. Here we return to the initial quote in that you are not asking simply how you can motivate the pupils you work with but how can you create the conditions in which pupils will motivate themselves? Perhaps in discovering a way you can do this, it would be useful to examine your day-by-day, lesson-by-lesson and moment-by-moment interactions with pupils; for important clues to pupil's learning preferences and behaviour can be hidden in the small details of everyday interactions. At this point let's look at an analysis of a lesson in terms of what the TA does or says in order to facilitate a pupil's sense of relatedness, autonomy and competence (Case Study 5.5). The TA in this example is working in a Year 7 class and though mainly supporting one pupil on the Special Educational Needs and Disabilities (SEND) register she is also circulating around the classroom.

Case study 5.5: An example of how one TA enables one pupil (Harvey) to experience autonomy, relatedness and competence.

Statements by the TA	Did the statement develop			Comments
	Autonomy	Relatedness	Competence	
You look cheerful today, did you have a nice weekend?		x		The TA is paying attention to the pupil, noticing how they appear and importantly expressing an interest in their life.
Do you need any help to get started on the worksheet?	x	x		The TA by asking the pupil if they want help is communicating to the pupil that they are in control and that they have a choice. This statement also demonstrates that the TA cares.
If you need me – put your hand up and I will get back to you, I am just going to see Jack.	x	x		Again the TA is assuring the pupil that they are there to support them if needed.
I saw your hand was up – thank you for being so patient in waiting.		x		The TA demonstrates that she was paying attention to the pupil.
I see you have made a start on your newspaper article and your first sentence is very powerful and really captures the readers' attention. I can see you have put a lot of thought into how you have written this.			x	Here the TA is making a comment in regard to the work they have completed both in terms of their effort and competence.
Now it is up to you how you would like to tell the story. Remember what the teacher said yesterday about planning an outline of what you want to say.	x			Here the TA is stressing the pupil has a choice in regards to how to proceed with the story.

Table 5.3 Levels of engagement and strategies

Pupil	Characteristics	Strategies (in no particular order)
Fully engaged	Intrinsic motivation Self-regulation Deep learning Growth mindset Good relationships with teachers and peers	Praise; encourages pupils to be the best they can be. If possible utilise Berger's (2003) ideas of producing multiple drafts (see p. 102).
Behaviourally engaged only	Participates Compliant- only does just enough Fixed mindset Anxious about challenges Surface learning	Praise; Encourage growth mindset (see pp. 140–141); Encourage emotional regulation (see p. 147); Develop study skills to promote deep learning (see p. 145).
At Risk	Does not participate Poor relationships with teachers/peers Learned helplessness Avoidance tactics Self-handicapping Lack of parental support	In interactions stress autonomy, relatedness and competence; Note any issues of concern and report to teacher and Special Educational Needs Coordinator; Determine individual praise style; In interactions stress autonomy, relatedness and competence; Support parents (see pp. 118, 127, 130)

Summary

Behaviour is complex. However, TAs have a very important role to play in enabling pupils to achieve. Earlier in this chapter we discussed how pupils could be classified in regard to being: fully engaged, behaviourally engaged only and at risk, and we noted that an aspiring to be brilliant TA would be working to support all pupils. Table 5.3 suggests possible strategies to use with each of these groups of pupils. Further details on these strategies are given in other chapters. Of course, these recommended strategies are in addition to following the schools policies and procedures and working effectively with other colleagues.

Remember you can make a difference!

Chapter 6

Relating to others

Introduction

When searching for an inspirational quote to start this chapter, which concerns relating to others in the wider school team and building professional partnerships, there were several choices – my favourite though was, 'Together Everyone Achieves More.' There are many advantages to working well in a team and we all like to consider ourselves team players, meaning that we work effectively together for the best outcomes for all. Working in a team means celebrating successes together and supporting each other when times are difficult. On your journey to become a brilliant TA you will be part of several teams ranging from the class team, of you and the teacher, the team of all support staff within the school, the Special Educational Needs and Disabilities (SEND) team and part of the wider school community, to include all pupils, staff and parents. You will meet professionals from a range of supporting agencies and you may work in a team carrying out set programmes from these agencies. Every day you will be in contact with teachers, pupils and parents and, therefore, you are an essential part of the complex web of interactions that make up the school environment. As such, you may be asked to give your opinion, written or verbal, about pupil progress and wellbeing. As a TA you have much to contribute!

In this chapter we will explore:

- interpersonal skills required for building positive relationships;
- aspects of working with teachers and parents;
- how to access information to help you within your role and to enable you to support others;
- the roles of supporting agencies.

Interpersonal skills required for team building

In Chapter 3 we discussed the importance of school values in promoting shared aims and creating a shared vision. If everyone is 'singing from the same hymn sheet', so to speak, the team is more likely to succeed. Team work relies on trusting and respectful relationships between teachers and TAs, and as Howes (2003) notes:

> effective teamwork cannot be easily subsumed into a relationship between leaders and led, when the process is as complex as teaching and learning in mainstream classrooms. Schools need to develop a concept of team working that is focused on the engagement in learning of all staff: this requires the development of trust over time ... Such a process emphasises critical reflection and casts everyone in the role of learner.
>
> (Howes, 2003, p. 152)

Discussion point

Ways to enhance teacher/TA partnerships

In conducting research for this book, with Foundation degree students, we asked what would enhance the teacher/teaching assistant partnership?

Replies included:

Ensuring that the progression of the children is the main objective;

Time to talk about the day, how things went and what is coming up;

The wish to be 'spoken to nicely by the Senior Leadership Team (SLT) and not to feel as if you are treading on eggshells' in your conversations with them;

When the teacher values you, your opinions and experience.

What do you feel are the highs and lows of working in a team?
List the essential qualities that you feel are needed for team working.

Teams in schools can be complex. Where schools promote and encourage lifelong learning for everyone in the school the overall team is more likely to be successful. The tone is often set by the Senior Leadership Team (SLT) and their attitude to the staff in their school. Team members will often have unequal amounts of power, with some members having the responsibility to make decisions and initiate change; nevertheless, everyone's opinions should be valued. As stated previously, it is important that everyone is 'singing from the same hymn sheet'; in order for this to happen it is important that everyone knows what is expected. Being explicit about roles and responsibilities can improve the effectiveness of teams. We will discuss this later in regard to Teacher/TA contracts (see p. 124).

When considering personal skills for good team players, in the previous discussion point, did you focus on skills such as the ability to listen carefully to others, to consider everyone's viewpoint, to negotiate sensitively, and for everyone to feel able to share their opinions? Developing good listening skills, questioning and extending others ideas, motivating others and developing others' skills and abilities are part of good teamwork. It also lies at the heart of effective teaching. Remember teaching and supporting learning is both a social and a team activity!

Emotional intelligence

Daniel Goleman popularised the term 'emotional intelligence' in his 1995 book of the same title. It can be defined as the ability to understand and manage your own emotions and influence those of other people. Developing skills to interpret how others may feel from what they say, their actions and their body language, in other words developing empathy, is a crucial human skill. Emotional intelligence is sometimes referred to as 'EI' or 'EQ' and there are many free online tests where you can assess your own emotional intelligence, providing that you answer the questions honestly! Related to the concept of emotional intelligence is self-regulation. Emotional self-regulation involves: the ability to deal with difficult emotions and feelings; the ability to calm yourself when you're upset or angry and cheer yourself up when you're feeling down or discouraged. Being a brilliant TA means that you can model emotionally intelligent behaviour for your pupils and help pupils to self-regulate their emotions.

Case study 6.1: Supporting Maddison

Jo, a secondary TA, was supporting Maddison in a Year 9 French class. In this class, Jo sat next to Maddison and as Maddison seemed to struggle in this lesson, Jo would often have to quietly repeat what the teacher said. Maddison seemed to need this as the teacher would often speak very quickly and Maddison could not keep up at all. During one lesson the class was particularly difficult to settle and the teacher yelled at everyone to be quiet. The teacher often did this; however, today the teacher also publicly singled out Jo, the TA, and said to the class, 'When I say be quiet I am also speaking to our TA, Jo.' Well Jo didn't say anything; she was mortified. Though she knew that she sometimes did speak in class at the same time as the teacher it was only to offer clarification to Maddison and she always made sure she said this in a very quiet voice.

If you were Jo, how would you react to this situation from the following?
Not say anything – after all you know this is just what this teacher is like.
Not say anything even if though you are very upset and angry. But you do go home, have several glasses of wine and spend most of the night worrying and in tears.
Confront the teacher after the lesson and give her a piece of your mind.
Do not say anything to the teacher but seek advice from your line manager on how to deal with this situation.
Other?

When discussing this hypothetical scenario (Case Study 6.1) with teaching assistants from a Foundation degree programme, several of these TAs were able to empathise with Jo having had similar experiences. Most had dealt with such situations by speaking with their line manager; however, resolution had not easily been found and the TAs felt that only by building a trusting relationship with the teacher and being allowed to feel part of a team would the situation improve.

Again, being a brilliant TA means being able to model emotionally intelligent behaviour under all circumstances. This as we all know and from Case Study 6.1, is not always easy. Keeping calm and employing emotionally intelligent strategies also requires practice.

When working as a TA there will be many times when you will need to help children to regulate their emotions when they are experiencing difficulties, such as feeling anxious about tests or when they have been involved in disagreements. As a TA you will want to be a calm role model on these occasions. You may need to offer support to teachers when they have had a difficult day. You may support parents who are experiencing difficulties or whose children have complex needs or challenging behaviours.

Discussion point

Self reflection

How aware are you of your own personal strengths and weaknesses in relationships at work?
Do you easily regulate your emotions?
How well do you respond to feedback? How well do you manage change?
How well does your school support staff and pupils to develop
an emotionally healthy school environment for all?

Working with teachers

When researching for this book we asked Special Educational Needs Coordinators (SENCos) studying for the National Award, at the university where we work, to characterise current teacher/TA relationships and describe what the ideal relationship would be in their school. They were asked to tick as many as relevant from the following:

- member of staff/line manager;
- friends;
- expert/apprentice;
- mentor/mentee;
- partnership of equals.

Encouragingly, 73 per cent of SENCos replied that their vision of an ideal relationship between teachers/TAs would be a partnership of equals and 68 per cent believed that this was already one of, or the only, main descriptor of teacher/TA relationships in their schools. Most SENCos were happy with current state of teacher/TA relationships in their schools, although several mentioned attitudes and personality as being factors that could make working partnerships difficult. This applied equally to teachers and teaching assistants.

When asked to list five essential qualities for the *ideal TA*, SENCos gave a range of different responses. Their top five responses were that TAs should:

1 Be able to use their initiative;
2 Understand how children learn;
3 Have personal attributes such as patience, approachability, being warm and interested in the child/young person's wellbeing;
4 Be a good communicator;
5 Have good subject knowledge.

As stated, the response that TAs should 'be able to use their initiative' came out on top. However, TAs could argue that not knowing what is required may be the reason why some TAs are not perceived as acting independently or using their initiative. In TA interviews for our research some mentioned being 'spoken to' by the teacher when having used their initiative in a way that they did not appreciate. It would seem that an ideal relationship depends on effective communication and agreement regarding roles and expectations. One way forward is to develop a teacher/TA contract as this can build your confidence and clarify the kinds of initiative your teacher wants you to employ.

The next most popular quality, or in this case a skill, was understanding how children learn. SENCos felt it was essential that TAs had a good basic understanding of how children learn in order to support them effectively. This is at the heart of what makes a good TA. This understanding involves knowing how and when to support pupils with their learning; appropriate questions to ask; knowing when to step back and allow pupils to engage with their learning independently and what constitutes effective praise and encouragement.

Many SENCos mentioned personal attributes such as patience, approachability, being caring and warm with an interest in children's wellbeing and their personal circumstances. One SENCo wrote 'friendly, warm and smiley.' These descriptions reflect the role of the TA in being the person that many pupils confide in or speak freely with.

The next quality was that of being a good communicator, with pupils and staff alike. Communicating with pupils to enhance learning requires understanding both how children learn and the optimum ways to promote learning through effective dialogue. Communication for learning is more than being open, receptive and empathetic to your listener.

When communicating remember that how you say something and your body language are as important as what you say (please refer to p. 71).

SENCos also valued TAs with good subject knowledge. Of course, this can be dependent upon good systems for sharing planning, with enough time for TAs to ask questions and seek clarification if they're not sure of lesson content or what their responsibilities are within the session. Having confidence to ask for support in areas that TAs may find challenging may be difficult; yet it is so important. It is better to say you don't know something than to give low quality support. Modelling 'not knowing' in front of pupils can be powerful for pupils who struggle. They often believe that everyone else knows everything and it is a good lesson to see that adults still need to learn and can admit to not knowing. Other qualities mentioned included charisma, creativity, reflective ability, being a good team worker and enthusiasm.

In exploring what makes for a great teacher/TA working relationship Bentham (2011) interviewed both teachers and teaching assistants and put forward a model of collaborative relationships (Table 6.1) based on their views. Of course you may have a completely different definition!

If you are a TA aspiring to be brilliant, a Teacher/SENCo reflecting on how to manage your team of TAs so that they are enabled to be brilliant or a Senior TA with responsibilities for working and training new TAs, you may after honest reflection acknowledge that there is room for improvement. In this case what can you do? Good practice in this area (Bentham, 2011) suggests a number of ways forward, for teachers and HLTAs working with new TAs, to include:

- *Play to strengths*, know what a TA excels at and know what they find difficult, never ask a TA to do to an activity that they are not skilled at or confident in;
- *Be an effective role model*, that is, be the educational professional you would like them to become;
- *Use selective praise and direction* to help them develop appropriate skills;
- *Encourage them to ask questions*;
- *Arrange appropriate training.*

Table 6.1 How Teachers and TAs defined and classified collaborative relationships

Type of Relationship	Great/Outstanding	Average Relationship	Awful/Poor
Personal attributes	High levels of trust evident which impacts on quality of communication and improves quality of provision to pupils. Trust enables Teachers/TAs to have more detailed discussions regarding how pupils learn and how they can learn from each other.	Trust developing, this trust enables Teachers/TAs to have basic conversations about pupil learning characterised by 'this child couldn't understand this', but important details are missing.	Absence of trust. Without trust relationships are perceived as stressful.
Planning	The ideal would be to plan with the year group staff to include teachers and teaching assistants. TAs would be involved in planning and could help teachers to plan, receive, suggest and share ideas.	TAs have some input but do not attend teachers planning meetings. TAs input characterised by 'adding in how we're going to deliver something, rather than coming up with ideas'.	No TA input or involvement in planning. TAs not listened to and ideas dismissed.
Feedback	TA feedback to teachers would focus on: aspects of pupil learning; strategies used; pupil achievements; discussions regarding where to go next and resources needed. Teachers would give direct constructive feedback to TAs and "both would be able to take criticism from each other and use it to improve".	Feedback regarding pupils was characterised 'by 2 or 3 minutes quick chat to talk about what they did, what they didn't get.' Teacher's feedback to TAs was general rather than being directive, that is, focusing on what children didn't understand, what TAs were doing and what TAs needed to do.	No communication
Real understanding of learning and stages (Teaching skills)	TAs would have good prior knowledge about the children and their learning and be able to use this knowledge to differentiate and adapt the material sufficiently within the learning outcomes if required to do so.	The TA had some knowledge and was still making a positive difference in classroom.	Lack of TA understanding resulted in pupils suffering in that pupils' learning was not being moved on.

Source: Bentham, 2011 Bentham and Hutchins, 2012, p. 71.

Discussion point

Defining relationships

How do you define a great working relationship?

To what extent do you agree with the proposed model outlined in Table 6.1?

What is your definition of an effective/ineffective teacher/TA working relationship?

Would somebody be able to come into a classroom and through observation alone say: 'yes that is an effective Teacher/TA working relationship?'

On what basis would they be able to make this judgement?

What would they see? What would they notice?

If I draw a line from one to ten, with ten being best teacher/TA relationship and one being a truly poor working relationship – where would you place yourself?

1	5	10

How do you move from one point to the next?

(Adapted from Bentham & Hutchins 2012, p. 70)

Case study 6.2: How do I support my teacher to support Shaun?

Shaun is a profoundly deaf child who attends a mainstream school. Though the school has a support centre for children with hearing impairments, Shaun is included in the classroom for much of the day. The teacher, a newly qualified teacher (NQT), finds it difficult to respond to Shaun's unpredictable behaviour. Some of the children in the class find his behaviour frightening. He can be volatile and his mood changes quickly. His communication difficulties along with a complicated home background, and possible attachment issues, make him anxious and in need of a great deal of support.

Shaun also receives support from both the specialist teacher for children with hearing impairment and the SENCo.

The TA in the class knows Shaun well and has a good relationship with him. She has taken time to observe Shaun and to look for potential triggers to his outbursts. She has kept some notes to look for patterns. She has noticed that his behaviour is more volatile on Monday mornings and Friday afternoons. Further, Shaun becomes very agitated in maths lessons. The TA realises that Shaun needs more visual prompts with his learning than he is currently receiving. On one recent occasion Shaun has thrown a chair across the classroom, narrowly missing another child.

The TA knows that the new NQT is struggling with Shaun, but the TA readily admits she has not yet established a close working relationship with the new teacher.

The TA want to help the new teacher and of course Shaun. The TA strongly believes she has much to offer but she is unsure how to do this.

What would you advise?

Time

Unsurprisingly both the SENCos and TAs, in the research carried out for this book, reported that having more time for communication is the factor that would most enhance the quality of teacher/teaching assistant partnerships. This is a recurring theme within the literature (Blatchford et al., 2012; Blatchford et al., 2013) and in our professional observations in school. Having time to discuss and share planning, give feedback and pass on information are still key issues in schools. Solving the problem of making the best use of the time available relies on *shared systems* between teachers and TAs being used effectively.

TA deployment policies

Good practice in deploying TAs means that schools should have a set of good practice guidelines in the form of a TA deployment policy for staff to follow. This should cover general issues such as what TAs may do to support pupils in general terms; for example, specifically how they should promote inclusion or respond to pupils' learning needs or deliver interventions. The TA deployment policy should outline what the TAs can do to support teachers; for example, providing administrative support or preparing resources if appropriate. It should include guidance on how TAs give support to the whole school at playtime or lunchtime. As a TA you should be familiar with this document which may also include your job description.

Case study 6.3: Our school's TA deployment policy

The SENCo, in discussion with all the TAs in their secondary school and referring to relevant guidance (Sharples et al., 2015), drew up a list of recommendations for best practice. The aim was to distribute this to all the teachers, ensuring that teachers understand best practice is essential.

Recommendations:
Use small group interventions wherever possible. Research shows this is the most effective use of TAs.

Ensure consistent communication between TAs and teaching staff. Find time to talk! Try and avoid 'snatched conversations.' Create your own 'shared systems' of communication that work for you.

Have meaningful interactions with TAs in lesson. Treat your TAs with respect.

Adapt seating plans to include TAs where necessary.

Ensure that all staff in the room are aware of priority pupils and strategies to best support them.

Apply school policies consistently with priority pupils.

Team Teach, that is, communicate effectively with TAs in regard to intended outcomes and progress.

Be clear on the TA's role. Supporting pupil(s) is the priority in this school! Remember it is the policy in our school not to ask TAs to undertake photocopying, marking and admin work.

Remember teaching assistants have an invaluable role to play in our school and when used effectively can have a major positive impact on pupil learning!

Do you have such a list in your school? What does your list say?
If you don't – what should it say?

(Courtesy of: The Forest School, Horsham, West Sussex)

Teacher/TA contracts

The most important relationship in school for many TAs is with the class teacher that they support. Day-to-day work in the classroom can require more detailed information than what is written in your average TA deployment policy. It is essential to recognise differences in the style of TA support that individual teachers require in their classroom. Policies may give fairly specific guidelines, however personalities also play a part. Having a 'contract' for TAs and teachers to negotiate can improve relationships, iron out difficulties and lead to improved practice for pupils.

Schools can devise their own checklists or contracts for teachers and TAs to go through at the beginning of the year, or when TAs change classes. Areas to consider include:

- *How to offer support in a particular classroom.* What are you expected to be doing within the lesson introduction, whole class work, group work or in the plenary? For example, in some schools there are systems for TAs to support 'carpet time' through the use of visual reminders rather than needing to verbally interrupt the session.
- *How should you deal with behaviour incidents?* Some teachers prefer to deal with most behaviour incidents themselves or in a particular way, others like the TA to intervene. As a TA you need to know what your role is.
- *In your classroom when the teacher asks* you 'to use your initiative', what does this mean?
- *How should you move around the classroom during sessions?* For example, who needs the most support, how should support be delivered and how does the teacher want you to meet targets such as promoting pupil independence?
- *What systems, written and oral, for sharing planning and giving feedback are in place?* For example in some schools the use of 'Post-its' or communication books are used to give teachers valuable information on pupil progress.

Explicitly agreeing on issues with individual teachers will clarify working practices for teachers and TAs. This may lead teachers to consider more fully the role that they want their TA to have and further help teachers to consider the impact and importance of the TA role. What is included in this teacher/TA contract will vary from school to school and possibly class to class, but it is good practice to give time to these discussions. After such discussions TAs then know what is expected in each classroom and can also share this information between themselves.

Discussion point

Reflecting on contracts

The Teacher/TA contract

Discuss with a colleague

Can you think of a time when it would have been useful to know exactly how the teacher wanted you to intervene or work with a child?

Have you ever felt unsure about what your response should be?

In your experience, to what extent do individual teachers vary in their expectations of your role?

Would a contract help? What would you include in a contract?

Working with parents

TAs have an important role in liaising with parents, though it is paramount to be professional in all communications and interactions. Remember if there is any criticism or complaint you must refer the parent to a teacher or member of the Senior Leadership Team.

On those occasions where parents choose to give you information, or feel more comfortable in, talking with you then remember the importance of being both a good communicator and a good listener. When communicating professionally it is helpful to utilise active listening skills to include:

- Be aware of the way that you are projecting yourself – your stance, amount of eye contact and non-verbal gestures;
- Pay close attention to the listener. This takes practice and may benefit from rehearsal. Use nods and 'fillers' such as 'mmm,' to encourage continued dialogue;
- Repeating back what someone has said is helpful in both making sure that you have fully understood and communicates to them that you are indeed listening;
- Be careful not to step in too quickly and close down a discussion or discourage a parent from continuing with what they want to say;
- If a parent discusses a problem with you respond without great shows of emotion, keep calm and refer them to someone or some resource (i.e. the Local Offer) that could help;
- In the same way that you would pass on information from a child do not keep secrets with parents, but offer support from other professionals where appropriate. Tell them that you will discuss

options to support them with other colleagues and that someone will get back to them.

Parents who choose to seek your help are already engaged with the school. However there are many parents who find communicating with their child's school very difficult. This group of parents referred to as 'hard to reach' are a diverse and complex group, with differing backgrounds and needs, many of whom may only have in common a distrust or fear of schools and the education system. They may include homeless families, refugee or asylum seekers, travellers, parents with learning difficulties or mental health problems, parents whose own experience of school was negative and those disaffected and disengaged with society. Some parents may perceive TAs as more approachable than teachers, and building good relationships by being open and friendly can help to build parent confidence. Giving parents positive messages and comments about their child's engagement, behaviour and progress can be a good foundation in welcoming them into the school. Parents of children with behaviour difficulties will be appreciative if you notice and report on times where their child behaved well in addition to the times when things have gone wrong. All parents appreciate hearing good things about their children so part of your role can be to pass on achievements and positives from the school day.

Many schools may utilise Family Link Workers or Parent Support Advisers whose role is to foster good relationships and support parents in managing behaviour and involving them in their child's learning.

Discussion point

Supporting parents

Talking with parents

Joe's mum, Ms Jones, seeks you out before school starts and says that she has been very cross with Joe and that they have parted on bad terms. Joe has wet the bed again, the washing machine is broken and she can't afford the repair. Ms Jones is very upset because she knows that shouting at Joe just makes things worse and that he doesn't wet the bed on purpose. She asks you to keep an eye on Joe. You know little about her situation, but agree to look out for Joe.

What would you do with this information?
How can you support Joe and his mum?
Who else may need to be involved?

Parents of children with SEND

It is important to understand the range of feelings that parents go through when their children are diagnosed as having special educational needs. Parents may first experience a range of feelings from guilt, shock, denial, grief, anger and sadness (Logsdon, 2018). However, with time there comes acceptance, relief and all the other joys and sorrows associated with having children.

In schools, we may engage with parents on the basis of supporting and teaching their child and assume that because the diagnosis has been in place for some time they will have processed these feelings. We may have only known them as a family with a child with SEND, however their expectations for family life may have been very different prior to their child's diagnosis. For the family coming to terms with their child's needs it may seem a relatively recent occurrence. People take varying amounts of time to process their feelings and may experience guilt and high levels of anxiety for some years. They may grieve for the child they had expected to have and whilst loving and doing their best for the child they do have (Logsdon, 2018). Be sensitive in your communication with parents. If a child is diagnosed during their school years, for example with dyslexia, language impairment or autism, parents need accurate information about the child's condition and possible interventions. They need to adjust to a new perception of themselves and their child. It is essential that parents be given an opportunity soon after diagnosis to go over the information and ask questions of the professionals. From the parent's perspective, getting the balance right between being overwhelmed by professionals who tell you about your child and receiving enough support can be difficult (Kisler and McConachie, 2010). Judging the needs and reactions of families requires sensitivity and the use of active listening skills by school staff.

Parents of children with SEND may need extra support at times of transition which can be very difficult. Uncertainty about the next transition or placement is common. Changing classes within the same school can be stressful for child and family. This can also be a difficult time for TAs. You may make close relationships with families and individual children and find it hard when children move on to their next TA. It is generally accepted as good practice that children should not become reliant upon one TA and that they should be encouraged to make new relationships and realise that a range of people can support them when necessary. This leads to greater independence for the child but can have its risks and downside for parents who need to get to know yet another professional. Reasons for changing TAs should be shared with parents and promoted positively. Although you may find it a challenge to move on from a rewarding working relationship with a child and family; the long-term interests of the child should be kept in mind. In some cases it may be appropriate to support a child for longer than the school year. This will depend on the judgement of all of the professionals involved with the child.

Case study 6.4: Supporting Eloise

You have supported Eloise for two years since she started in the Reception class. Eloise has Down syndrome. You have attended several courses about Down syndrome on how to promote language skills and reading with this group of children. You have a friendly and positive relationship with the family. You feel that you have just started to make progress with Eloise's reading skills using your specialised knowledge. Your SENCo tells you that another TA will be supporting Eloise next year. The family is not happy about this and want you to continue to work with her.

What should your professional response be to this scenario?
How will you discuss this with the parents?
How does this make you feel?
How can you best support Eloise and the family?
Importantly how can you share your knowledge with the new TA?

In regards to Case Study 6.4 on Eloise, as a brilliant TA you will want to support the colleague who takes over your role by sharing your knowledge of Eloise and the family, for the benefit of all. Outlining how you have communicated with the family, what you have learnt about Eloise and Down syndrome, and being available to support the new TA will demonstrate your flexibility and professionalism.

The SEND Local Offer

In the *Special Educational Needs and Disability Code of Practice: 0 to 25 years* (2015) the government outlines their expectations for every local authority to publish a Local Offer. The SEND Local Offer is intended to be a source of information for parents, young people and professionals, outlining what support is available in the area for all pupils with SEND, not only those with an Education, Health and Care plan. Schools publish their school offer as part of this, outlining their special needs provision and any particular expertise they can offer and this is regularly updated. The process of keeping an up-to-date Local

Offer is intended to improve provision. Reviews and comments can be left by users of the SEND Local Offer regarding specific provision, website information and accessibility. The Local Offer should explain the role of education and health professionals and be a source of current information to include a list of services available from the local authority and the voluntary sector. For example, West Sussex County Council SEND Local Offer links states:

> Visit our one-stop shop for services for children and young people with special educational needs and/or disabilities (SEND). Our 'Local Offer' website brings together services, information and events available for children and young people with SEND and their families.
>
> (WSCC, 2018)

By clicking on the SEND Local Offer link a range or further resources and information are presented to include: SEND Activities, Transport & Travel, Finding Support, Keeping Safe, Money Matters, Activities open to all and Early Years and Schools.

Activity 6.1 Using the Local Offer to make a difference

Undertake an online search for your Local Offer – this will help you to be able to support parents to find it. Spend some time exploring the website. Look up any areas that interest you, follow links to support groups and activities. Find the section on your school and see what your school says it can offer children with SEND. Then complete the following:

Jade and her family have recently moved to the area. Jade is on the autism spectrum and has found the move difficult, but is starting to settle into school well. Jade's mum confides that she (mum) is struggling to make friends in the area and is feeling increasingly isolated. Jade's dad works long hours and mum seems depressed. You try to involve Jade's mum in school life, encouraging her to come and hear readers, which is having a positive effect. You spend half an hour investigating the Local Offer and are able to give Jade's mum some suggestions for support, for meeting other people and for holiday support.

Question: Investigate the Local Offer for your area online as if you were the TA in this scenario. What did you find? How accessible was the Local Offer? What would you suggest to Jade's mum?

Other professionals

Services have a statutory duty to work together to safeguard children. Multi-agency working has expanded enormously and in many areas education, social and health services are co-located. These professionals work as part of a multi-agency safeguarding hub providing support for children and their families. As such, referrals for families should be made quickly and the level of support required assessed by these multi-agency teams.

Families who may have debt, housing, drug and alcohol problems or domestic violence issues should be able to receive targeted multi-agency support. Programmes such as *Early Help* and *Think Family* (WSCC, 2016)) are there to support the early stages of problems and hopefully resolve issues before situations escalate to crisis levels. There are a variety of roles associated with this type of parenting and social support details which can be found on most Local Offers. *Family Link Workers, Parent Support Advisers, Think Family Keyworkers* are some of the job titles you might discover when investigating the Local Offer. School staff such as SENCos and *Learning Mentors* may play a role in planning support for families.

Pupils with mental health difficulties may need referrals to the Child and Adolescent Mental Health Service known as CAMHS. Child and Adolescence Mental Health Service teams include nurses, therapists, psychologists, support workers and social workers as well as other professionals. The role of CAMHS is to assess and treat young people with emotional, behavioural or mental health difficulties such as eating disorders, anxiety, depression and self-harming.

The role of an *educational psychologist* (EP) is primarily to assess learning needs and advise schools on good practice in managing behaviour and learning needs. Educational psychology is an educational support service and EPs are responsible for large groups of schools. Educational psychologists can help schools to provide interventions by training staff for example in 'Precision Teaching' (a specific system for one to one teaching to acquire fluency and mastery of skills or knowledge) or emotional wellbeing and resilience. Educational psychologists will contribute to Education Health and Care Plans (EHCPs) and their review.

Other services provided by local authorities are the *behaviour support service* and the *social communication team*. Behaviour support advisors and the social communication team often provide training and support and programmes for both pupils requiring support and their parents.

Clinical psychologists may provide counselling, therapy and advice to individuals and their families through Child and Adolescent Mental Health Services (CAMHS) or general practitioners (GPs).

Speech and language therapists (SALT) have an important role in school as the number of children with language delay and disorder at school entry continues to rise (Nasen, 2017). The role of the SALT is to provide training for schools in how to improve language skills, to assess pupils and provide programmes for schools to carry out. Some schools will have a designated TA to do this work who has received extra training.

Referrals to occupational therapists (OT) can usually be made by schools or GPs, for children who need support to perform everyday activities and physical skills such as dressing, eating, sitting and handwriting. Children may have conditions such as dyspraxia or cerebral palsy. Occupational therapists can suggest exercises, equipment and adaptations, for example particular pencil grips or special chairs. They may provide programmes of exercises to improve core stability (building muscle strength to support the ability of the torso muscles for good posture and balance) or hand control. You may engage with other professionals, such as *sensory support* teams, for children with hearing impairment or visual difficulties. You may encounter some or all of these professionals depending on your role in school. They can enrich your own professional development and are a valuable source of information and ideas. Using other professionals as a resource can only support you on your journey to become a brilliant TA.

Summary

Working effectively in a team and relating well to others are key skills for becoming a brilliant TA. As a TA, you may as part of your role, work with a range of professionals, and have the opportunity to develop positive working relationships that will benefit both pupils and your own continuing professional development. Demonstrating those much-valued 'kindly qualities' of being 'warm, friendly and smiley' to those you work with in school will be appreciated by pupils, parents and professionals who are all a part of your school community.

Chapter 7

What is best practice?

Introduction

In Chapter 1 we discussed the role of TAs from a recent historical perspective and in doing so highlighted numerous reports and research documents. From our historical outline it was apparent that how to use TAs effectively in schools has been discussed by both practitioners and researchers over many years. However, one clear question has emerged and that is: How can the impact of teaching assistants be maximised?

To begin to answer this question a number of research projects, guidance and books are relevant, these include:

- Deployment and Impact of Support Staff (DISS) report as detailed in the book *Reassessing the Impact of TAs: How Research Challenges Practice and Policy* (Blatchford et al., 2012);
- *Challenging the Role and Deployment of TAs in Mainstream Schools: the Impact on schools* (Blatchford et al., 2013);
- Education Endowment Fund *Making Best Use of Teaching Assistant Guidance Report* (Sharples et al., 2015);
- *Maximising the Impact of Teaching Assistants* (Webster et al., 2016) and;
- *The Teaching Assistant's Guide to Effective Interaction* (Bosanquet et al., 2016).

This chapter aims to review relevant research in regards to what is seen as best TA practice and to outline recommendations in a form that is both easy to understand and implement. It is easy to get overwhelmed by the sheer amount of guidance or advice that is out there; as such, we hope that this chapter will equip you with some strategies that can aid in your journey to becoming a brilliant TA.

Recommendations

In order to make sense of all the guidance offered, perhaps it is first helpful to recall the old saying: *'Grant me the serenity to accept the things I cannot change, the courage to change the things I can and the wisdom to know the difference.'* As a TA it is not within your power to change educational policies and legislation in this country or to take it upon yourself to re-write your school's behaviour policy; but as an aspiring to be brilliant TA you can make your views known and you can make a difference to the lives of the pupils you support. As a starting point Table 7.1 and Table 7.2 outline recommendations from key reports and asks you to reflect on the current practice within

Table 7.1 Reflecting on recommendations from the Deployment and Impact of Support Staff (DISS) report and the Wider Pedagogical Role Model. (Blatchford et al., 2012)

Responsibility	Factor	Recommendations from DISS Report in regards to best practice	What is the current practice in your school?
What can TAs do?	TA practice	Prioritise pupil learning over task completion. Take a proactive approach to the role. Ask questions and utilise talk that opens up discussion.	
What can the senior leadership of schools and individual teachers do?	TA deployment	Teachers are responsible for the learning of each pupil in their class. Interventions and activities, for individual pupils and groups, carried out by the TA need to be planned and monitored by the teacher. Not separating pupils from teacher and mainstream curriculum.	
	Preparedness	Train teachers to work with and/ or manage TAs. Create opportunities for the teacher and TA to have the time to plan, prepare and feedback. Develop TA subject and pedagogic knowledge.	
	Conditions of employment	Do not rely on the goodwill of TAs and other support staff. Incorporate good line and performance management processes.	

Table 7.2 Reflecting on, *Making Best Use of Teaching Assistant Guidance Report* (Sharples et al, 2015)

Responsibility	Recommendations from Guidance Report in regards to best practice	What is the current practice in your school?
Every teacher in everyday classroom context.	TAs should *not* be used as an informal teaching resource for low attaining pupils. Use TAs to *add value* to what teachers do, not replace them. Use TAs to help pupils develop independent learning skills and manage their own learning. Ensure TAs are fully prepared for their role in the classroom.	
Use of teaching assistants in delivering structured interventions out of class.	Use TAs to deliver high quality one-to-one and small group support using structured interventions. Adopt evidence-based interventions to support TAs in their small group and one-to-one instruction.	
Linking learning from work led by teachers and TAs.	Ensure explicit connections are made between learning from everyday classroom teaching and structured interventions.	

your school. Of course what is apparent in these recommendations is that, in order to maximise the impact of TAs on pupil learning, everyone to include senior leaders, teachers and TAs needs to work in collaboration.

Recommendations are great, but in order for recommendations to become reality there is a need to understand what each recommendation looks like in practice. So, in no particular order let's look at the recommendations from a variety of perspectives.

What can Headteachers and senior leaders do to maximise the impact of TAs?

In regards to the Headteacher and the senior management team there is specific guidance to:

- train teachers to work with and/or manage TAs;
- not rely on the goodwill of TAs and other support staff;
- incorporate good line and performance management processes.

Though the task of TAs is to support pupils within the classroom, there are important caveats. In Chapter 1 we discussed the *Special Educational Needs and Disability Code of Practice: 0 to 25 years* (DfE, DoH, 2015) which clearly stated that:

> teachers are responsible and accountable for the progress and development of the pupils in their class, even where pupils access support from teaching assistants or specialist staff.
>
> (Paragraph 6.36, p. 99)

As a TA it is important to remember that teachers are responsible for:

- the learning of each pupil in their class;
- ensuring that pupils are not separated from themselves (the teacher) and the mainstream curriculum and that;
- TAs should not be used as an informal teaching resource for low attaining pupils.

Again these recommendations are seen to address past criticisms where the most vulnerable and needy pupils were seen to be supported by staff with the least qualifications. No TA should ever be put in a situation where they feel they have been 'thrown in the deep end', that 'they are making it up as they go along' or that they and the pupils they support are isolated from the rest of the class. Of course one of the recommendations to emerge from the Effective Deployment of TAs (EDTA) project (Blatchford et al., 2013) was that TAs should be deployed to work more often with middle and high-attaining pupils while teachers worked with low-attaining and SEN pupils.

Further examples of best practice include:

- using TAs to deliver high quality one-to-one and small group support using structured interventions;
- schools adopting evidence-based interventions to support TAs in their small group and one-to-one instruction;
- ensuring explicit connections are made between learning from everyday classroom teaching and structured interventions.

It is the role of the teacher to ensure that TAs are fully prepared for their role in the classroom and that teachers need to create opportunities for themselves and TAs to plan, prepare and feed back on learning activities. This is an issue of communication and in Chapter 6 we discussed examples of Teacher/TA contracts (p. 124), the importance of finding time to talk and to share views (pp. 125–125) and models of what makes for great collaborative relationships (p. 121). In the next chapter we will discuss examples of interventions and joint training.

What can TAs do to maximise their impact on pupil learning?

After reflecting on the responsibilities of teachers and senior management teams we now focus on aspects of good practice that you, as an aspiring to be brilliant TA, can develop. These include the ability to:

- deliver high quality one-to-one and small group support using structured interventions;
- prioritise learning over task completion;
- take a proactive approach to the role;
- acquire and develop subject and pedagogic knowledge;
- ask questions and utilise talk that opens up discussion;
- help pupils develop independent learning skills and manage their own learning.

Delivering structured Interventions out of class

The research (Alborz et al., 2009; Sharples et al., 2015) states that one of the best ways to deploy TAs in schools is by involving them in structured intervention programmes. An intervention programme is a set of activities that is designed specifically for pupils perceived to have challenges or to be behind in certain areas of the curriculum, for example, in maths, handwriting or reading. There are currently a range of structured interventions such as: Catch Up, Numbers Count, Reading Recovery, Springboard, to mention just a few. Running structured interventions are now a core responsibility for many TAs. Typically, interventions are delivered away from the teacher and the classroom and as we note best practice (Sharples et al., 2015) involves the teacher and TA finding the necessary time to discuss progress and ensure that explicit connections are made for the pupil between learning that occurs during the intervention and learning that occurs in the classroom. And of course best practice would necessitate that TAs are given the training and support to run these interventions.

Externally sourced structured interventions, created from research, often stipulate certain steps or activities in a certain order; the instructions of such interventions need to be followed explicitly. These structured interventions have been successful because of these factors, so the advice is don't change them as changes or alterations could dilute the effectiveness of the intervention.

Mindset

In terms of best practice one way of enabling pupils to learn more effectively and efficiently, according to Carol Dweck, is by encouraging students to adapt a growth mindset. Mindset reflects an individual's belief about how ability and effort are related; if pupils in schools believe that their brains can grow and change then this has a profound influence on their attitude towards learning. A pupil with a growth mindset who believes that intelligence can be developed through effort will confront challenges, learn from mistakes, try new approaches and persevere in the face of learning challenges. Such pupils know that putting in the effort and trying new approaches are ways of becoming smarter. In contrast a pupil with a fixed mindset will believe that an individual has a certain amount of ability and therefore effort will not really make a difference; you either have ability or you don't.

Many schools now label themselves as *growth mindset communities,* but Carol Dweck cautions that a growth mindset is not a destination but rather a journey.

In revisiting her work, Dweck (2015, 2017) notes a number of common misperceptions and ways forward to include:

- A growth mindset isn't just about effort! All those working with pupils should praise effort *but only if effort is connected with actual learning.* Therefore if a student is struggling but not understanding it is not helpful to say, 'Great effort! You tried your best!' as this communicates to the pupil that they are actually not very good at learning. Rather educational professionals should discuss with the pupil why they are struggling and what other approaches they could take, for example, 'Let's talk about what you've tried, and what you can try next.'
- Be aware of the false growth mindset! This is where an individual (parent, teacher, teaching assistant) may claim that they have a growth mindset and work with pupils to encourage this; but their actions do not match their words, that is, they can 'talk the talk but not walk the walk.'
- We should **not** see individuals as either having a growth mindset or a fixed mindset rather we should recognise that we all are a mixture of fixed and growth mindsets and most likely will always be so! If an individual wants to move closer to a growth mindset it is important to first acknowledge our fixed mindset thoughts, actions and feelings. Have you ever worked with a pupil who has said, 'I have made a mistake and I know that mistakes are an opportunity

to learn but actually I feel awful'? Or perhaps you have had that experience yourself. Carol Dweck (2015, 2017) is recommending that both on a personal level and to help our pupils we need to:

- look out for 'fixed mindset' triggers, that is, events that trigger a response of feeling useless, anxious or incompetent;
- become aware of these negative patterns of thoughts;
- accept these thoughts in order to challenge them, that is, talk back to these negative thoughts with a growth mindset voice;
- remember growth mindset is not an end point but a journey.

Discussion point

Encourage a growth mindset

Reflecting on mindsets

Think of a time when you have found something difficult to learn, maybe learning to drive, learning to ski, taking up knitting, reading academic articles or learning and remembering a new idea or word.

Did you have a fixed mindset reaction? Did you engage in negative self-talk?

Did you feel incompetent? Did you look for an excuse? Did you become defensive or angry?

Here we need to listen to Dweck's advice of accepting those negative fixed mindset thoughts and feelings in order to challenge and work through them.

One way of doing this is talk back to these negative thoughts with a growth mindset voice?

When you find things difficult and are ready to give up what do you say to yourself?

How could you support pupils to do this?

Take a proactive approach to the role

One recommendation in regards to best practice states that TAs need to be proactive. We have highlighted a number of ways in which this can be accomplished within the chapters in this book, they include:

- Being clear about teacher's expectations. For example, we recommend that you talk to the teacher at the beginning of the year to clarify, 'What can you do?', 'What can't you do?' and 'When there are episodes of challenging behaviour what would the teacher you support like you to do?'

- As TAs may be a first point of contact for families it is important that the TAs support the school proactively in sharing the school's ethos and values;
- Request support or training if you need to. Brilliant TAs are pro-active in seeking development and training opportunities;
- One proactive means of promoting behaviour for learning is to find ways of motivating the pupils you support or better still finding ways to create the conditions in which the pupils will motivate themselves.

Discussion point

Not waiting to be asked

In what ways are you proactive?
In what way could you be more proactive?

Developing subject knowledge

As part of the Teaching Standards, teachers are expected to have a secure knowledge of the relevant subject(s) and curriculum areas. Teachers are expected to be able to foster and maintain pupil's interest in the subject and address any misunderstandings or misconceptions the pupil may have. As a TA, supporting pupils' learning, having an understanding of relevant curriculum areas is crucial. In school you will be supported by your teacher who will discuss with you the lesson plans and your role in implementing them.

Case study 7.3: How much subject knowledge does a TA need?

Sarah was working with a Year 5 class where they were discussing the 'War with Troy.' Sarah was supporting a group of high ability pupils who were required to listen to a podcast on the War with Troy and then to consider what makes for a hero in ancient Greece.

At the end of the day Sarah discussed the session with her mentor.

Sarah: If you're doing literacy and the teachers says – well next week we're doing the 'Trojan War' or whatever the relevant topic is. Well, I honestly don't know a lot about the War with Troy; it would be nice to be able to have that time to find out information. Because when the children ask you a question you think well actually I don't know, you know, and sometimes you have to say, 'I don't know, let's find out together', which is fine and a good teaching strategy but for me I just think it would be nicer to have that time to do some research on the topic. The teachers, they know what they're doing because it's in their heads already, they know it. Well, I get to see the lesson plan the week before and maybe it is just me, but I don't think it is enough time.

If you were Sarah's mentor what would be your advice?
How much involvement in the lesson planning do you have?
Would having more time to research curriculum topics enable you to better support pupils?

In interviews with teaching assistants Bentham (2011) found that though some TAs had lesson plans in advance TAs thought there would be advantages to being both more involved in the planning and having additional time to think and further develop their knowledge on the topic. In Case Study 7.3 the TA realising that she couldn't answer a pupil's question is using a recommended strategy of working with the pupil to 'find out things together.' Though this strategy would lend itself to encouraging independent learning, the issue reflected in the incident concerns how much more the TA felt she could support pupils in their learning if she had more involvement in planning and time to think and learn underpinning subject knowledge. Perhaps as a brilliant TA this is an issue you will need to discuss with the teachers you support.

Developing pedagogic knowledge

Simply pedagogy is the discipline that deals with the theory and practice of education; it concerns the study and practice of how best to teach. Pedagogy involves what teachers/TAs do (actions), what they know (knowledge and understandings) and why they act as they do (underpinning beliefs about the value of education and how children learn). Re-phrased, pedagogy involves reflecting on 'how I teach', or 'how I support learning' so that 'those I teach or those I support, learn.'

One way forward is the role of talk, or what is referred to as 'talk for learning', 'the power of classroom talk' or 'dialogic teaching.' Dialogic teaching builds on the theories of Vygotsky in that we learn within a social context and that through talk we build shared understandings. As Alexander (2017, p. 2) states:

> although student talk must be our ultimate preoccupation because of its role in the shaping of thinking, learning and understanding, it is largely through the teacher's talk that the student's talk is facilitated, mediated, probed and extended – or, all too often, inhibited.

The quality of pupil/teacher or pupil/TA talk can be examined at a number of levels as Table 7.3 outlines.

Classroom talk, managed and modelled by teachers and teaching assistants, has the power to develop pupil understanding and as such best practice recommends that TAs pay great attention to the moment-by-moment conversations they have with pupils.

Table 7.3 Levels of talk (adapted from Alexander, 2017, p. 5)

Levels of Talk	Focus	What is required
Collective	The classroom as a site of enquiry and joint learning.	Teachers, TAs and pupils discuss the learning tasks together.
Reciprocal	Pupils listen to each other, share ideas and consider alternative viewpoints as a part of the classroom activities.	Many classrooms will use 'talk partners' where pupils come together to discuss and share their views. Some pupils will need support in regard to how to talk together.
Supportive	This describes the nature or quality of the conversation.	Pupils should be able express their ideas freely, without risk of embarrassment over 'wrong' answers. Here we recall the nature of a growth mindset and the role of the teacher/TA in encouraging this.
Cumulative	This highlights how ideas are developed with participants building on their own and each other's contributions in order to develop coherent lines of thinking and understanding.	Teaching professionals can support development of shared understandings and higher thinking skills in pupils by their considered use of questions and responses to pupil answers.
Purposeful	That classroom talk is carefully managed and structured with specific educational goals in mind.	Teaching professionals will have learning objectives in mind and be able to foster learning in both structured and informal settings.

Asking questions and utilising talk that opens up discussion

A key recommendation for schools wishing to maximise the impact of teaching assistants is to train TAs in the ability to effectively utilise talk and questions. Here the aim is to move away from an educational practitioner who merely sifts through pupils' answers looking for the 'correct answer' to a practioner who treats each pupil's question or response as an opportunity to extend pupil thinking and knowledge.

In order to do this Nystrand and colleagues (1997) state that consideration not only be given to the specific questions to ask but to how you will respond to pupils' answers. For example, one way to move the pupil's thinking forward is to build on their replies and to incorporate what they have said into further questions.

But, what constitutes an effective question? Questions are used as a strategy to support learning. Questions are asked for a number of reasons, to:

- Check for understanding or find out what pupils already know or how they are thinking about what they have been asked to do. To specifically check that pupils understand instructions, processes and concepts;
- Review and revise previously taught material by recalling what they have learned and making specific references to prior learning so as to help pupils consolidate or reinforce memories;
- Promote focus and task engagement;
- Encourage thinking, and to encourage pupils to ask questions themselves;
- Gain pupils' attention and make sure that pupils are listening;
- Draw in shyer pupils.

(Brown and Wragg, 1993, Nystrand et al., 1997,
Blatchford et al., 2013)

Work on questioning has revealed that there are different types of questions. One dimension of questioning is referred to as open versus closed (or narrow versus broad). These dimensions describe the types of answers that are required from the pupil. For example a closed or narrow question would be: 'What is the capital of Iceland?', to which there is only one correct answer. On the other hand, an open or broad question would be 'What did you do on Christmas day?' Obviously there are no right or wrong answers and answers could be quite short or very lengthy and elaborate. Another dimension of questioning is referred to

Table 7.4 Types of questions

Type of Question	Knowledge Required	Example
Requires recall	Narrow	What is the capital of Iceland?
	Broad	What did you do over the Christmas holidays?
Encourages thought	Narrow	Do you think the story had a happy ending?
	Broad	What do you think would be an exciting ending for the story?

as recall versus thought. Recall questions check on existing knowledge and observation, while thought questions stimulate the development of new ideas and in that respect create new knowledge. It is also important to consider whether the questions are clear and easily understood; that is, do the pupils understand what they are being asked? The manner, or tone of voice, in which the questions are asked is also important. Are the questions seen as an opportunity to participate in a stimulating classroom discussion or are they a means of catching out those pupils who are not paying attention? There is an art to questioning. A good questioner will match the style of their questions to the demands of the lesson and the characteristics of the learner (Table 7.4).

Further, Brown and Wragg (1993) identified a number of common errors in questioning including:

- Asking too many questions;
- Asking a question only to answer it yourself;
- Not giving pupils enough time to think about the answer to a question. It is always important to allow sufficient wait time;
- Always asking the same pupils;
- Asking too easy or too difficult questions;
- Not responding to wrong answers;
- Ignoring answers;
- Failing to build on or link pupils' answers to questions.

Discussion point

Closed or open questions

Do closed questions have their place?

At a recent INSET day, as a group of TAs we had a session on effective questions. One TA asked the consultant who was running the session, 'Are closed questions always 'wrong' to use and must we always avoid them?' Well the consultant did not answer the question directly but divided us into groups and asked us to discuss a suitable response.

Though most of us thought that open questions were always better as they stimulated and encouraged thinking, one experienced TA argued that closed questions had their role in promoting learning or helping pupils to scaffold their answers.

The TA gave us the following example of a recent conversation she had with a pupil:

TA: Which do you think is heavier, the large balloon or the small marble?

Pupil: I don't know?

TA: Is the balloon the same as the marble?

Pupil: No

TA: How are they different?

Pupil: Don't know?

TA: Are they made up of the same material?

Pupil: No

TA: So what are they made of?

Pupil: The balloon has air inside and rubber on the outside – and the marble is glass.

TA: Right – so what do you think is the heaviest?

As the experienced TA explained, open questions are great in encouraging thinking but sometimes closed questions are a good way to build up or scaffold thinking skills or simply to encourage the pupil to start talking and thinking. Giving some pupils an easy question gives them the confidence to then say more. Hopefully in time the pupil will be able to internalise the questions and use these questions to think for themselves when they are problem-solving.

How would you reply to the question: Are closed questions always 'wrong' to use and must we always avoid them?

Benjamin Bloom outlined a classification system of thinking skills ranging from lower order to higher order cognitive skills. Bloom's original classification system or taxonomy was first published in 1956 but then revised by Anderson and Krathwohl (2001). In the classroom Bloom's revised taxonomy (Table 7.5) is often discussed in terms of types of questions or activities that can be used by teachers/TAs to develop thinking skills in the pupils they support.

Table 7.5 Bloom's revised taxonomy

Level of thinking (from lowest to highest)	Definition	Examples of instructions related to levels of thinking. Pupils are asked to:	Examples of questions TAs can ask.
Remember	To learn pupils must first store information in their memory, or to be precise their long-term memory and then be able to recall or retrieve this information when needed.	List Recall Recite Remember Define Memorise	In regards to the story... Where did the story take place? Who was the main character? How old was the boy when he went to sea?
Understand	The next level of thinking refers to making sense of facts. Can pupils explain the ideas?	Discuss Explain Describe Report Identify Summarise	How could you summarise the story?
Apply	Applying involves using or implementing this knowledge in a new context or way.	Demonstrate Illustrate Solve Use Interpret	In the story the boy learned to conquer his fear of swimming. Now that he had learnt this strategy how can he use this new strategy to solve other problems? How could you use this strategy?
Analyse	Breaking knowledge into constituent or smaller parts. Can pupils distinguish between the different parts?	Differentiate Compare Contrast	The story of Joe going to sea is quite long. If you were to divide the journey into chapters what would they be?

Evaluate	Making judgments against criteria and standards through checking and critiquing material. Can a pupil justify a decision?	Judge Assess Criticise Argue Defend	Let's look at the example of a previous pupil's essay. What was good? What needed improvement? What level would we give it and why?
Create	Can a pupil create a new product, application or view?	Invent Innovate Design Construct Formulate	Write a poem about going on a voyage.

Source: Adapted from Anderson and Krathwohl, 2001; Fredricks, 2014.

Case study 7.4: Brilliant TAs are involved in training new TAs – Planning a training session on Bloom's taxonomy

Antonia, an HLTA in a primary school, was asked to talk to the new TAs in her school about Bloom's taxonomy. Antonia, after researching the area, discusses her plans and detailed notes for the session with the SENCo.

Antonia: First I will talk about the importance of questions. Questions should be used to teach pupils and not just to check what they know – that is to test them. We use questions all the time, I looked this up online and found an article that stated: 'Teachers ask up to two questions every minute, up to 400 in a day, around 70,000 a year, or two to three million in the course of a career' (Hastings, 2003).

SENCo: Amazing – perhaps as a pre-sessional task you could ask the TAs to record how many questions they ask in one day.

Antonia: Then I plan to talk about the history of Bloom's taxonomy. Educators such as Benjamin Bloom argue that children's thinking skills are developed by the questions they are given. Therefore higher levels of questioning are needed in order for pupils to think at higher cognitive levels. Bloom's original classification system or taxonomy was first published in 1956 but has now been revised by Anderson and Krathwohl (2001). The levels, from the lowest to the highest, are Remember, Understand, Apply, Analyse, Evaluate and Create.

SENCo: I am sure the new TAs will find this very interesting. Having a handout about the different levels and the questions to use at each level would be helpful for new TAs.

Antonia: I then plan to talk about how using questions can help students consolidate their knowledge of facts and why knowledge and remembering is important. To learn pupils must first store information in their memory, or to be precise their long-term memory, and then be able to recall or retrieve this information when needed. Being able to remember key facts is important! Indeed Willingham (2009) argues that individuals who have more facts stored in their long-term memory learn more easily and that knowledge of facts is more important than imagination, as you need to have knowledge before you can imagine. Willingham (2009, p. 45) stated that knowledge is 'a prerequisite for imagination, or at least for the sort of imagination that leads to problem solving, decision making and creativity.'

SENCo: I can see you have really researched this area. I think this would be a very useful discussion. It is very easy to look at the levels and just assume that the higher levels of thinking are more important. Yet to think at higher levels you need to have the necessary knowledge or facts to make this possible – which is what both Bloom and Willingham are talking about.

Antonia: To help the group understand Bloom's taxonomy and make sense of these levels of thinking I am planning to ask them to reflect on how they have used this.

SENCo: That is a really good idea. Perhaps it would be useful to ask TAs to work in their year groups and consider examples of different questions they ask the children and to match this to the levels.

Antonia: I could ask the new TAs to record the questions they have used throughout one day and bring this to the session.

SENCo: That is a good idea. Perhaps you could also ask the TAs how they could have extended the children's thinking by asking different questions. I think this will be a very useful session. The handouts you have prepared reflect your extensive reading, includes references and ideas for further reading. Well done!

Much information and advice has been presented regarding questions. Activity 7.1 sets out to test your knowledge and understanding of questions.

Activity 7.1 What type of question is it?

Question	What type of level of thinking does the question call for? (Remember, Understand, Apply, Analyse, Evaluate and Create)	When would you use this question?	What type of question is this? (Open, Closed, Recall, Thought)
What is the first sound in the word?			
Can you count the syllables in the word?			
What questions would you ask if you were interviewing the Prime Minister?			
Can you think of a word that rhymes with this word?			
What does the word mean?			
What was the underlying theme of the story?			
Do you believe there is life on other planets?			
Can you think of a word that means the opposite?			
Can you use the word in a sentence?			
Is the word a noun, verb or adjective?			

Enabling pupils to manage their own learning

One of the key concepts discussed in Chapter 4 was the concept of scaffolding and the zone of proximal development. To recap, scaffolding was defined as the process by which learners are supported to achieve learning goals and to be able to carry out tasks independently or as Woolfolk et al. (2007, p. 73) states, scaffolding requires:

> giving information, prompts, reminders and encouragement at the right time and [in] the right amount, and then gradually allowing students to do more and more on their own.

The zone of proximal development refers to the difference between what a pupil can achieve alone and what they can achieve with help. As educational professionals when supporting pupils it is first important to establish what they can achieve independently, what they can achieve with a little support and what they can achieve with much support.

When discussing lesson plans with a teacher, the teacher may use certain terminology such as: learning objectives, learning outcomes, success criteria and process success criteria (see Table 7.6).

Process success criteria

When discussing pupils' progress the teacher will want to know whether a pupil has achieved their learning objective(s) and importantly 'how they got on.' For example the teacher will want to know how much support did they need, could they do the task independently, did they require extension activities or were there were any misconceptions or misunderstandings. As outlined in Table 7.6 success criteria explain *what* is to be achieved while process success criteria relates to *judgments* on pupil progress in regards to *how* they have achieved. These judgements on '*how they got on*' can relate to both the whole task or the components, or mini-goals, that make up the task. Being able to break a complex task into bite size chunks or mini-goals enables you as the TA to give detailed feedback on pupil progress in relation to each part of the task.

Imagine the following:

The learning objective for an activity is to write a short paragraph of at least four sentences.

Let's imagine the success criteria for this activity is to:

- use a capital letter at the beginning of each sentence;
- use the correct punctuation mark at the end of each sentence;
- write sentences that are related to one another.

Table 7.6 Learning objectives, Learning outcomes and success criteria

Terminology	Definition	Pupils will want to know:
Learning objectives (Product)	This outlines what the pupils will have learned within the session, that is, what they will able to do at the end of the session that they could not achieve at the beginning.	What are we going to learn?
Learning outcomes (Process)	This refers to what *activities* the pupils will do in the session.	How are we going to learn?
Success criteria (product)	This outlines *what has to be achieved.* The success criteria is often presented as *a list* of activities or steps that a pupil needs to do in order to successfully complete the task or learning objective.	How do we know if we have succeeded?
Process success criteria	This refers to the steps or mini goals that make up the task. At this point the teacher/TA is observing the pupil to see **how** they are doing on the task or **how** are they doing on each mini-goal or component of the task.	What steps do we need to take to achieve success and *how* do we need to do this? To become an independent learner the pupil will need to be able to self-evaluate their success on each component or mini-goal of the task.

Source: Adapted from: Bosanquet et al., 2016; Clarke, 2014.

Imagine that you are supporting a small group of pupils and at the end of the session all pupils have written a paragraph. Yes, the teacher will be pleased but the teacher will also want to know 'how the pupils got on', that is, the teacher will want to discuss the *process success criteria*. So for starters the teacher will want to know for each part of the task if the pupil could do this:

- independently;
- did they need a bit of help and if yes what type of help did they need;
- did they require extensive support and again what type of support was required?

This level of detail in regard to feedback will enable both you and the teacher to track pupil progress. Teachers will need to know this information to inform their planning. Likewise as the goal is to enable the pupil to ultimately achieve independently what they can only initially do with help or support, it is important to involve pupils in assessing their own work. Therefore part of your role when working with pupils is to enable a pupil to 'know what steps they need to do to complete the task' and 'what type of work is needed to reach a certain level or grade.' Further, as part of your role, you can encourage pupils to make connections between the effort they put in, their appropriate use of strategies and how both relate to their learning outcomes. The realisation, that 'what I do can make a difference' is essential for the development of a growth mindset.

To provide effective pupil support and feedback a TA needs to be able to 'break' any learning task into mini-goals. The more abstract a task the more difficult this may seem. However, there are a few tips you can use to ensure you fully understand the success criteria *that is, the list* of activities or steps that a pupil needs to do in order to successfully complete the task. These tips include:

1 It is best to access the planning prior to the lesson to give you a head start on identifying tasks or learning objectives, that need to be broken down into mini-goals;
2 If this is not possible, then take the time while the teacher is presenting the tasks or learning objectives, to break down the task into mini-goals for the pupils you support;
3 Then take the opportunity to clarify your understanding of lesson objectives and mini-goals with the teacher, while the pupils are getting their books or going back to their chairs.

Help pupils develop independent learning skills

Paula Bosanquet, Julie Radford and Rob Webster (2016) in their book, *The Teaching Assistant's Guide to Effective Interaction* outlined a scaffolding framework for TA-pupil interaction or 'five steps teaching assistants must follow to increase student independence.' The scaffolding framework was outlined in the book with Webster (2017) further describing this framework in an article entitled: 'The five steps teaching assistants must follow to increase student independence'.

An effective TA is one who is not constantly interacting with pupils. Instead, they are allowing them to try things for themselves, observing their progress, and only intervening for a specific reason.

(Bosanquet et al., 2016, p. 46)

Table 7.7 Scaffolding for independence

Level of Support	Step	Strategy to Be Developed	Abilities of the Pupil	The Role of the TA
Highest level of independence Lowest level of support from TA	**FIRST STEP**	**Self-scaffolding:** TA's default position is to observe how pupils' are doing and to give pupils the time and space to think and try the task for themselves.	Here the pupil is an independent learner. The pupil has the strategies to engage with the task and manage their own learning.	First you need to stand back. If you ask a pupil a question you need to be silent and wait for them to respond. If the pupil is required to get on with an activity you might say: 'Off you go' or 'Try it yourself first.' Again, give the pupil time and space to think.
	SECOND STEP If a pupil is struggling then you need to offer support but only just enough. Again, allow the pupil time to think.	**Prompting** If pupil is 'stuck' offer a nudge.	The pupil is engaged in their own learning.	As a TA you might say, "What do you need to do first?' What's your plan?' It is important to note that at this stage you are not giving the pupil specific information.
	THIRD STEP If a pupil is still struggling then you need to offer support, but only just enough. **Support needs to be drip-fed.**	**Clueing** If a pupil cannot remember what to do offer the smallest piece of information, that is a hint, to enable the pupil to move forward.	The pupil is engaged in their own learning.	The hint will be specific to the task. If you were helping a pupil write a sentence and they were struggling with punctuation, you might say, 'What do we need to remember when we come to the end of the sentence?' Again allow time for the pupil to process and think about the information and if necessary give another hint.

FOURTH STEP When a pupil genuinely does not have the strategies or skills to complete the task then these need to be taught.	**Modelling** If pupil has no idea what to do, a TA can model the activity for the pupil.	The pupil is still actively engaged in their own learning.	A TA may say: 'Let's do this together' or, 'Watch me do this first, then it will be your turn.' Within this approach utilise knowledge on effective questioning and talk.
FIFTH STEP TO BE AVOIDED	**Correcting** If, in correcting a pupil, the TA provides the pupil with all the answers and is not requiring the pupil to think or re-think their answers then the pupil is not learning.	The pupil is **not** engaged in learning.	If a pupil writes 2 + 2 = 5, A response of 'No that is not correct, the right answer is 4', will not help the pupil realise their mistake or to learn how to add.
Highest level of support Lowest level of pupil independence			

Source: Adapted from Bosanquet et al., 2016 and Webster, 2017.

Of course as a TA your moment-by-moment interaction will also depend on your knowledge of pupil abilities, that is, your knowledge of the pupil's zone of proximal development. As we remember, the zone of proximal development refers to both what a pupil can do independently and what they can do with help. As a TA you will need to provide, through the process of scaffolding: the right type of support, the right amount of support, and deliver this at the right time. As the goal is to enable the pupil to ultimately achieve independently what they can only initially do with help or support, you will also need to know when **not** to offer support. So here we need to think in terms of levels of support required for the pupil to meet their learning outcomes. However in providing support to encourage pupil independence Bosanquet et al. (2016) recommends that it is advised that a TA 'needs to work to the rule of providing the least amount of help first', (p. 60) and 'if necessary offer more, but only just enough to enable them to achieve the task' (p. 59) (see Table 7.7).

Case study 7.5: Recording progress

Sharon, a TA, was working with Jodie on writing paragraphs.

I know from previously working with Jodie that she can do most of the steps or mini-goals involved in this activity, though sometimes she can get confused between punctuation marks, for example between a full stop and a question mark. Jodie was asked to write a short paragraph on what she did over the Christmas break. I initially tried a 'try it yourself first' approach with Jodie. Below are some notes I made after our session to discuss with the teacher.

NOTES

Success Criteria	Scaffolding for Independence	Process Success Criteria How did you evaluate pupil's progress on component tasks or mini-goals?
Use a capital letter at the beginning of each sentence.	Can do this independently	When I came back to Jodie she had written four sentences, all starting with capital letters and all relating to each other.
Can write sentences that are related to one another.	Can do this independently	

Use the correct punctuation mark at the end of each of the sentences.	Modelling	After her first try all sentences ended with question marks where no question marks were needed. I tried giving her a prompt and then giving clues allowing for her to have time to think, but Jodie just stared blankly. I then reviewed with Jodie the difference between question marks and full stops. We then worked through some examples together and then I asked Jodie to look back at her work and to correct her work. Jodie could now do this. At the end of the session, I praised Jodie saying, 'you worked really hard, you put in a lot of effort and you wrote four sentences with the correct punctuation – Well done!'

Keeping a record of Jodie's progress is helpful for her, the teacher and myself!

We have presented much information on what constitutes best practice within this chapter. Though the ideas to include: growth mindset, effective use of questions, scaffolding and scaffolding for independence may seem easy and straightforward, putting them into practice is complex. An aspiring to be brilliant TA needs to reflect on the use of such strategies as Case Study 7.5 illustrates.

Case study 7.6: A little bit of knowledge is a …

Omar, the HLTA, was asked to observe Lettie, the new TA.

Lettie was working in a Year 5 class and Omar watched Lettie circulating around the classroom offering praise to all the pupils. Lettie would always say with a great smile on her face, 'Great Effort!', 'Well done!' and it was clear that the pupils adored Lettie's enthusiasm. However, Omar also noted that Lettie tended to offer praise unconditionally even to the pupils who had clearly not been engaged in the learning or had achieved very little during the whole session.

One student, Jonas, was really struggling and Omar noticed Lettie going over to Jonas and saying, 'You have a go first.' Jonas replied, 'I can't do it' to which Lettie replied, 'You mean you can't do it yet.' Lettie continued to circulate offering much praise again not connected to learning and then came back to Jonas. Jonas had not even started the task. Lettie then said, 'Well – What do you need to do first? – you can do this.' Lettie then moved on to circulate around the other pupils. At this point Jonas got up, threw his books across the classroom and stormed out.

After the session Omar and Lettie met to discuss how things went.

Lettie: I really don't know why Jonas got so angry. I was following all the advice encouraging a growth mindset and scaffolding for independence. I truly believe in the importance of a growth mindset and I made a point of praising everyone for their effort.

Omar: Yes, but the difficulty is that while scaffolding for independence and encouraging a growth mindset are great approaches and seem easy to implement – both are actually more complex and in the reality of the classroom other factors have to be taken into account. Praise for effort always needs to be connected to learning. We need to be aware of how pupils could interpret what we say. If we say 'great effort' and the pupil knows they haven't tried they might think that we have really low expectations of them. We should always work towards enabling pupils to become independent learners; however, we must always work within a pupil's zone of proximal development, that is, asking a pupil to do work that is for them, 'doable but challenging.' When Jonas said he couldn't do the task perhaps he really couldn't. Also when working with pupils such as Jonas we really need to be aware of other factors; you know that Jonas' grandmother recently died. Supporting pupils' learning is challenging but at the same time we are in a very privileged position. Having a growth mindset is just as important for us as it is for the pupils we support and you have the potential to be a great TA.

Summary

In this chapter we have reviewed current advice and guidance. Being brilliant involves being able to put together all this information such that you are able to offer the right amount of support, the right type of support and at the right time. This is not an easy task but to enable you to achieve this you will need to make the time to have meaningful discussions with your teacher and/or more experienced TAs. In order to rise to the challenge of supporting pupils you need to ask questions, engage in reflection and take on constructive feedback.

Chapter 8

Using best practice to make a difference

Introduction

TAs work best as part of a team and often the job of a TA involves working with others to implement policy initiatives, programmes or interventions. Approaches to education are always evolving and naturally schools wish to incorporate these new approaches into existing practice. For example, TAs could be involved in initiatives regarding phonics programmes or ways to enhance emotional regulation or to foster growth mindsets.

In Chapter 3 we discussed the graduated approach, a model of action and intervention which aimed to implement effective special educational provision and that this model of action or support takes the form of a four-part cycle, consisting of Assess, Plan, Do and Review. This chapter will discuss in further detail the TAs' potential role in implementing and evaluating initiatives, be they designed for the whole school, whole class, small groups or for one individual pupil. These examples are inspired by real experiences of TAs, and will build on the advice given in Chapter 7 regarding best practice.

Each case study will start with a brief outline of the initiative before describing the role the TA played in delivering the intervention, collecting the necessary evidence and feeding back to others. But before case studies are discussed an aide-memoire will be given regarding what an aspiring to be brilliant TA needs to know about any intervention.

Aide-memoire: The basics of any intervention

Step 1: Rational/Justification

When introducing a change, in most cases, a reason or justification is given. If the change is in the form of a whole school initiative often the change is introduced via INSET sessions for the staff team and sometime whole school assemblies. Often the staff member leading the intervention will refer to recent research, an inspiring conference presentation, an influential book or sometimes all of the above. In other cases the rationale for an intervention results from analysis of school data or perhaps an Ofsted report. On a whole-school level perhaps there has been an increase in challenging behaviours, or it is seen that mental wellbeing is an issue, or the attainment gap between children and young people from economically disadvantaged backgrounds and their fellow students is now a school priority. On an individual basis perhaps an assessment of progress indicates that some pupils are seen to be in need of SEND support.

Step 2: The plan

The intervention, or change, will often require relevant staff members to alter their existing practice and incorporate new ways of working. If the change involves direct TA involvement in regards to a specific structured intervention for an individual or a small group such as: delivering phonics sessions or a maths programme then specific guidance and training must be given before the intervention begins (see p. 137).

It is key that all relevant staff have a shared understanding of what this new practice entails and specifically what their involvement in this new practice is, before the intervention begins. It is important that all those involved ask questions to make sure that they 'know what they should be doing.'

Step 3: Success criteria

Most of the time interventions will stipulate success criteria at the beginning of the programme. Success criteria describes what needs to be achieved and is often presented as a list. Simply, success criteria outline the means by which everyone will know whether the programme has worked. Examples of success criteria could include:

- pupils' achieving a certain grade or level or mastering a certain skill;
- teachers and TAs perceiving they have more quality time with each other to discuss pupil progress;
- existing good practice in one department within a school being disseminated to other departments.

In order to measure success, evidence will often be collected prior to the intervention, sometimes this is referred to as baseline data after the intervention has finished. What evidence needs to be collected will depend on the nature of the intervention and should be understood by everyone involved before the intervention begins.

Step 4: The doing phase – Implementing interventions and collecting the evidence

All those involved in the change will need to know their role both in delivering the intervention and in collecting evidence. For example you may be asked to:

- watch a pupil in class and make notes of what they are doing (collect evidence);
- you may be asked to work with a small group on a new phonics programme (participate in the intervention), write up notes on individual progress and to make general comments on how the session went (collect evidence).

From the perspective of the TA it is always good practice to discuss with the teacher/SENCo or relevant educational professional before you begin delivering the intervention. It is important to know how you are required to present the evidence. Is there a special form you need to fill in? How much detail is needed? Are there any specific factors you need to comment on? Asking for an example of how they wish you to record information is always helpful.

Step 5: Evaluating, reviewing and moving forward

At a designated time those involved in leading the change or intervention will want to know whether the intervention has worked or not. If the intervention is for groups of pupils they will want to know whether it *has worked* for all or just for some pupils and importantly they will want to know *why* it has worked. Likewise if the programme *did not work* it will be important to determine *why* this happened. This information, consisting of the analysis of feedback and data collected, is key to informing the next cycle of action or further future interventions. Your opinion is valuable and it is important that you have the confidence and ability to engage in honest reflection regarding your participation in the intervention.

Case study 8.1: Jayne's tale of joint CPD for teachers and TAs on engaging disengaged pupils

I work as a TA in a large secondary school supporting pupils in the English department. Over the course of the year I was involved in joint CPD with teachers and TAs in our department. Every three weeks we would all meet up and have input on motivational theory and practical applications to use in the classroom.

As part of the CPD activity the English teacher I support, Mrs Diego, and I were asked to focus on one specific pupil who we thought had *'motivational challenges.'*

Research says that CPD works best if from the outset there is a specific target and success measures are specifically outlined.

As such we were asked to answer the following questions:

* Who is your selected pupil?
* What is this pupil like now?
* Where would we like him/her to be in six months?

In addition the teacher and I were asked to compile information on our selected pupil, Calvin, in regards to his achievements to date, issues with behaviour and attendance and what we perceived to be his barriers to learning. Importantly we also asked the pupil for his views. This was where the intervention became very interesting. It was very clear that though the teacher and I both agreed he was the least able in the classroom, if not in his year group, and that he had real behavioural issues; when we asked Calvin how he perceived himself as a learner – Calvin thought he was doing just fine. That was a real surprise for both the teacher and myself. Did he really think he was doing well? Was this just bravado? This made us both reflect. As part of the CPD – we started to compile detailed records of what Calvin was doing in the classroom and then in the CPD sessions we had time to reflect on what we had found out and how it compared to various motivational theories. We talked a lot about effective praise in the classroom and realised that we had been giving him lots of praise but sometimes for just writing the learning outcomes from the board. Perhaps Calvin truly believed that he had done well in the lesson if he had written just one line down. The real breakthrough came when we were discussing Dr Green's views on learning. Dr Green in his 2009 book *Lost at School* said: 'Challenging kids already know how we want them to behave. They are already motivated. However, kids with behavioural challenges lack important thinking skills' (p. 10). As we were discussing this in class I remembered a specific incident when I had asked Calvin to take his work to the teacher to have it checked. Strangely he came back to his desk and just kept looking at his work and said, 'well it is still here.' At the time I had taken no notice of this but in talking this over with the teacher I realised that actually Calvin did not understand what the phrase, 'Go check your work' meant.

The teacher agreed and stated that by the time students arrived in Year 9 she had assumed that they would understand what 'checking your work' involved. However acknowledging Calvin's lack of understanding was a breakthrough. The teacher asked if I could put together a study skill programme for Calvin, which I did and we were amazed at the difference this made. Participating in joint CPD made a real difference for one pupil in our class. At the start of the programme we agreed that we would know if we were successful with Calvin if he was engaged in the learning process and if he made an effort in class. Well now Calvin makes a real effort in class and is not just writing one line but writing paragraphs. Why did this intervention make a difference? The motivational theory was interesting but perhaps more importantly by doing this training together the teacher and I were speaking the same language so to speak, and by meeting every three weeks for joint CPD sessions we had real quality time to discuss and reflect on the pupils we worked with and in Calvin's example what we needed to do to move his learning forward.

What did I learn from this that I would tell an aspiring to be brilliant TA?

Participating in a joint training programme with teachers and TAs was great! If you have the opportunity to participate in joint CPD take it.

Reflecting on what would move a pupil forwards is important and reflecting on this with your teacher is invaluable. At first I was not confident to tell the teacher my opinions but now I realise just how much I have to contribute and how much the teacher values hearing my opinion.

Always get the pupil's perspective. Often they surprise you!

(Bentham, 2016)

Case study 8.2: Jo's tale of teaching emotional regulation strategies

I work in a large primary school in an area of social economic deprivation. In our school 60 percent of the children attending are entitled to Pupil Premium funding and we have a high number of pupils on the SEND register, with many children having behavioural challenges. Consequently the school has decided to implement a whole-school emotional regulation intervention.

At the first INSET day of the year, our SENCo explained:

> As you will all know our school has a large number of children across the year groups who lack resilience and who have heightened emotional reactions to small issues. For example, some children become very upset or extremely angry at the slightest provocation. As a way of helping all children to develop emotional regulation, that is, the ability to 'calm themselves down' when they get upset or angry or 'cheer themselves up' when they become discouraged, we have decided that as a school the focus this year will be on teaching emotional regulation strategies. We will aim to teach all children ways of rating their problems and rating their responses to problems. We all have had experience of children who with the smallest amount of provocation lose control and find themselves removed from the class. When this happens children fall into a negative cycle of acting up and sadly come to believe that they can't succeed at school. Further by being sent out from the classroom they can begin to feel that they do not belong at school and that learning is not for them.

I found this INSET day and the research on emotional regulation very interesting as I had worked with several children who just seemed unable to deal with their emotions. For example, I once asked a pupil (Jason), why he threw a chair across the classroom at a fellow pupil and he simply replied, 'He took my pencil.'

Our SENCo stated that the programme would involve the children:

- being explicitly taught how to rate their *problems* on a scale from one to five, with five being a really massive problem and one being a minor issue;

- being encouraged to discuss both examples of problems they face on a day-to-day level in the classroom and ways of resolving these problems;
- being explicitly taught how to rate their *responses to problems* on a scale of one to five, with five being a massive response and one being a minor response. The principle of this intervention is that the *level of the response to the problem* should equal that of the *problem size*. So a minor problem should result in a minor response;
- being taught specific skills and strategies to reduce an overreaction and self-soothe. For example, children will be taught some basic relaxation techniques involved in mindfulness. Specifically children will be taught to regulate their breathing patterns, which has a calming effect on heart rate and stress responses;
- being taught 'cognitive restructuring' of negative thought patterns, consistent with cognitive behaviour theory. Children will first be taught to distinguish between negative and positive thoughts and techniques for changing negative ways of thinking into positive ways of thinking. An example of a negative thought pattern would involve the child saying or thinking that they are 'useless'. We will want to help children to replace these negative thoughts with positive thought patterns such as, 'I can't do this yet, but I am getting better.' The SENCo recommended Tina Rae's (2016) book *Building Positive Thinking Habits*.

The delivery of these strategies will be included during weekly sessions throughout the year. Further, four whole-school assemblies will be given to teach and consolidate the strategies and all staff will be encouraged to use the strategies when dealing with disruptive and challenging behaviours. In addition, every class and group room will have an emotional regulation display to remind pupils of strategies.

Obviously it was very important that everyone in the school was on message and that we all supported the strategies. Of course what the SENCo didn't say at the first session was that all these discussions regarding rating problems and responses to problems, recognising negative and positive thoughts and restructuring or changing negative thoughts into positive thoughts had to be discussed in a manner that the individual child would understand. The teacher and I discussed in great detail how this would work in our classroom and the teacher specifically asked me to work with Jason. Together we discussed a way of working with the child, collecting evidence and evaluating progress and by the end of the year that pupil had really improved. At the beginning of the programme we talked about what success would look like for Jason; to begin with, he would fly off the handle for almost no reason. Therefore we felt that success for Jason would involve Jason learning how to manage his emotions. We realised that the programme had worked for Jason when he told me that another child had taken his pencil but that as this was a small problem and needed a low-level response he was reporting this to me.

Did the programme work? Well it certainly worked for the pupil I supported. Why did the programme work? Well – I think we very much personalised the intervention to the pupils we were working with. Also I think everyone was very clear on how the intervention worked and that it was important we were all singing from the same hymn sheet.

What did I learn from this that I would tell an aspiring to be brilliant TA?

It is very important to really understand what the intervention involves before you start. At first I was slightly confused with the terminology. Cognitive behaviour theory and cognitive restructuring are not terms I use every day. I did ask my teacher several times to please go over what I was supposed to do. Though I was hesitant to say I was unsure what to do, the teacher was really pleased that I was honest enough to say so.

As part of the intervention the teacher asked me to take observation notes on the pupil. But again I wasn't sure what she meant me to observe. So for the first few times we undertook the observation at the same time and then compared notes. This was really helpful as I came to understand what the teacher wanted me to look for and how much detail she needed.

Case study 8.3: Sharon's tale of joint practice development

I have worked as a TA in a special school, specifically in classrooms for children with autism, for over 15 years. Over this time I have built up a wide range of knowledge and experience that is recognised and valued by the senior leadership team.

This year, at our first INSET day in September, our deputy Headteacher explained that we as a school would be engaged in joint practice development. We were told that joint practice development (JPD) was more than sharing good ideas; it was about being responsible for working with others to implement great ideas in new settings and that this would be achieved through mutual observation and coaching.

The deputy Headteacher asked me to stay after the session and told me that Miss Rogers was going to be the new teacher in the specialist autism class, which I had supported for the last 15 years. Miss Rogers had limited experience of teaching pupils with autism and as a new teacher she did not know the existing structures and routines. This meant, as the deputy Headteacher explained, that the new teacher required support early on, mainly in the practical areas of how to structure the classroom and organise the learning as well as use of schedules, visual support and task layout. Once these aspects of practice were in place then Miss Rogers would be able to plan personalised and appropriate learning.

So the idea, according to the deputy Headteacher, was that Miss Rogers and I were going to be involved in joint practice development; so I, as the long-term TA, was being recognised for my great practice and I was going to work with the new teacher to implement these ideas in the classroom.

As the deputy Headteacher explained, rather than merely transferring my knowledge to the new teacher joint practice development allowed for the development and innovation of practice with both parties, that is, benefitting the giver and the receiver.

In order for joint practice development to work I would be meeting both with the new teacher to discuss class routines and the needs of the pupils, but also I was to have coaching conversations with the deputy Headteacher. These coaching sessions would allow me to reflect on the process of working with the new teacher and to learn through this activity.

To be honest, at first I was really unsure how this would work out. The deputy Headteacher explained that the new teacher would also be coached and that this would allow her to apply the knowledge she was acquiring to the specific pupils in the class.

Coaching conversation

During the autumn term I met with the deputy Headteacher for coaching about every two weeks. During our first conversation the deputy Headteacher asked me, 'how did I know' what the pupils needed. Actually that was rather difficult to answer as I knew them all so well. The deputy Headteacher stated that I instinctively met the pupils' needs and knew what they needed, but I needed to move my knowledge and experience from being tacit to being explicit – something which I could articulate and therefore share with the new teacher. This was a necessary first stage to ensure expertise could be shared.

Mutual observation and working together

The teacher and I worked together in setting up the classroom and organising the routines, including visual support. As we did this I explained to the teacher why I was doing what I was doing. Miss Rogers was eager to get going and to implement her own ideas. However, through the coaching conversation I knew it was my responsibility to share my knowledge of the pupils with the teacher. So sometimes I would say, for example, 'well before we do this with *Amy* she needs to have certain routines and structures in place' or 'when we work with *Jason* we really need to pay attention to the pace of learning.' I realised through coaching that I was not overstepping my position but that I had a key role to play in ensuring that the learning was appropriate for the pupils and that the pupils had the right provision in place.

The success criteria for this programme was that I would be able to share my good practice with the teacher in such a way that we both felt that we had learnt from the experience.

At our next INSET day the deputy Headteacher discussed progress of the JPD initiative and encouraged both Miss Rogers and myself to share our experiences.

When it was our turn to speak Miss Rogers talked about how much she had learned from my expertise. But when it came my turn to speak I realised that my practice had also changed through talking about routines and explaining procedures to Miss Rogers. The way the class ran was not the same as the last academic year. Indeed, through discussing classroom practices together we had developed new ways of working with the children.

The deputy Headteacher finished the INSET day, by saying:

> It is very easy for school staff to assume that the teacher is the one who should have all the answers. When there are TAs with a wealth of experience and expertise in a school it is important to enable them to play their part in supporting the development of new teachers and to contribute to the pupils' learning through sharing their practice.
>
> (Case study 8.3 inspired by: Petch, 2016)

What did I learn from this that I would tell an aspiring to be brilliant TA?

Though there may come a time when you instinctively know what to do, it is always important to be able to say *how you do it* so you can share your knowledge with others.

Coaching was a very useful technique to clarify my thinking.

When I first started working everything was so new and then there came a point when I realised I knew a lot and that I had a lot to offer. At the same time I found working with new teachers more difficult as I was unsure how much I could or should say. However I realise now that we all learn together and that I have a duty to share my knowledge with others in a respective and professional manner.

Case study 8.4: Manuel's tale of a growth mindset Initiative

Manuel has worked as a TA in a secondary school for several years. In the last academic year the school introduced a growth mindset initiative. As Manuel explained, growth mindset is our main ethos for all our teaching and learning. What this meant for our school was that all staff attended growth mindset sessions, we had regular assemblies and mind-set Mondays every week in tutor time. In addition, there are growth mindset displays across the school and the school has made changes in assessment strategies in regard to feedback and marking; this is where I am involved.

As a TA I support a number of departments to include History and English. In the lessons though I have certain pupils to support. I will often work in small groups.

In terms of working with pupils we now have clear guidelines in regards to our growth mindset initiative. The guidance we have is to encourage, 'I can't do it yet mentality' by:

- First helping pupils to recognise what they say to themselves when they are struggling;
- Helping them to acknowledge that we all have negative thoughts about ourselves as a learner from time to time but that everyone can learn;
- Offering second chances and drafting opportunities;
- Encouraging trials and failures;
- Correcting student attitudes about themselves by helping pupils talk back to their negative thoughts;
- Praising pupils for effort but remembering that we need to praise effort that is connected to learning;
- Giving pupils the space to reflect and form personal goals – what we call growth time;
- Giving timely feedback on effort and strategies;
- Personally modelling a growth mindset and talking with pupils about how we work through learning challenges;
- Remembering that growth mindset is not an endpoint but a journey.

Many of these points are on posters that are displayed around the school and in the classroom. As we work most of the time in small groups it is important to know how these guidelines specifically translate to how we actually talk to the pupils we are supporting. To help us to do this as a school we are encouraged to use such phrases as: 'Great effort! I like the way you tried a number of strategies before you solved the problem' or 'Great mis-take – An opportunity to learn – Now what strategy could you use next?'

In terms of establishing success criteria at the start of the year, in every subject we ask all pupils to fill in a form regarding where they see themselves in terms of a fixed or growth mindset and to explain why. For example one of the students at the beginning of the year filled in the form:

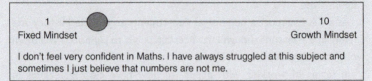

1 ——————————————————————— 10
Fixed Mindset   Growth Mindset

I don't feel very confident in Maths. I have always struggled at this subject and sometimes I just believe that numbers are not me.

This pupil's statement was typical of the many pupils I support. I knew by helping her to monitor her responses and by repeating this activity at specified times in the year I would be helping to provide evidence on whether our school's growth mindset initiative was working for pupils. I knew that my role in this initiative was to help pupils realise that they could learn, to encourage pupils to talk back to their fixed mindset thoughts and praise pupil effort when there was a link between effort and pupil learning. I knew it was hoped that these strategies would help pupils change their views of themselves as a learner.

From my point of view what was really helpful was that the teachers would meet with the TAs and ask us for our comments on how we thought pupils were progressing in regards to their view of themselves as a learner. The teachers would also observe us interacting with our groups and give us feedback on how we were supporting growth mindsets by the language we were using. One useful comment I received from the teacher was that I needed to *only praise pupil effort where learning had actually occurred* and to reflect on whether *my feedback was perceived as genuine* by the pupils I supported. This really made me think.

What did I learn from this that I would tell an aspiring brilliant TA?

From my experience of working in a school there have always been whole school interventions – but as a TA you have responsibility for making these interventions work on a one-to-one level with the pupils you support.

Again knowing what these interventions meant for me in my everyday interactions with pupils was important and receiving feedback on how effectively I used language to promote growth mindset attitudes was really important. I was fortunate that my teacher thought this was an important part of the whole school initiative. But I know in the past we have had whole-school initiatives and I have just been left to get on with it. Now I would ask the teacher for specific feedback on how I am delivering the intervention.

Summary

What has been presented in this chapter is case studies, inspired by real experiences, of TAs interaction in initiatives. Of course what makes this area complex is that initiatives can take many forms. But what is important is that TAs have a vital role to play in the success of these initiatives. In summary an aspiring to be brilliant TA will always:

- Clarify their role in the intervention;
- Ask questions if in doubt;
- Know what the success criteria is, that is, specifically know, *'how you will know if it has worked'* before the initiative starts;
- Know what evidence to collect and how the teacher wishes you to collect this information;
- Make time to feedback to the teacher;
- Ask the teacher or relevant line manager for feedback regarding your involvement in the intervention. Ask what went well and how your involvement could improve;
- Reflect on the intervention. For example, consider what parts of the intervention have worked, whether different strategies have worked for different pupils, how the intervention could be improved;
- Make your opinions known in a respectful, reflective and constructive manner.

Chapter 9

What does a brilliant TA look like?

Within this book we have presented much relevant knowledge and guidance that we hope an aspiring to be brilliant TA would find useful. Further, to encourage reflection we have included numerous case studies, activities and discussion points.

But perhaps, in conclusion, we need to return to the beginning chapters.

In writing this book we surveyed some of the TAs we work with in regard to what they thought was the way to brilliance. In their opinion, to be brilliant a TA needs to:

- Be prepared to constantly learn;
- Be able to adapt to your environment;
- Use your initiative;
- Always be open to new things and ideas;
- Engage in self-analysis and critique;
- Learn through trial and error;
- Observe and make a note of qualities in other TAs that you aspire to be;
- Develop confidence, engage in training and persevere;
- Build a good relationship with the teacher, this can be difficult at times because of work and time pressures, but it is worthwhile and very beneficial;
- Be clear about what the teacher's expectations are;
- Be organised, proactive and responsive. Remember you are the teacher's eyes and ears in the classroom;
- Work closely with the teacher. Develop good classroom management strategies. Get to know class routines. Be aware of the lessons plans. Think ahead regarding resources that are needed. Get to know your pupils well. Ensure support is available to the pupil when necessary but ensure that this support doesn't prevent pupil independence;

- Practice, read lots and ask lots of questions;
- Observe good practice and adapt your own working practice to match this. Remember you will continue to learn new strategies for dealing with situations as no one situation is the same;
- Be willing to help in any way you can and be prepared for any challenges you may face. Realise that no matter how long you are a TA there will always be challenges;
- Take on board advice and criticism;
- Start with a passion for wanting to help children and wanting to improve their outcomes.

Finally, in concluding this book we ask you to reflect on your own unique way to brilliance. Covey (2004) in his book, *Seven Habits of Highly Effective People*, argues that success requires a balance of both personal and professional effectiveness. In Chapter 1 we asked you the reader to specifically focus on Habit 2: Begin with The End in Mind. Stephen Covey on his website suggests that one way of doing this is to create your own Personal Mission Statement as this:

> focuses on what you want to be and do. It is your plan for success. It reaffirms who you are, puts your goals in focus, and moves your ideas into the real world. Your mission statement makes you the leader of your own life.
>
> (Covey, 2018)

So after reading this book what does your vision of a brilliant TA look like and more importantly, what is your personal mission statement, your personal plan for success?

Bibliography

Alborz, A., Pearson, D., Farrell, P. and Howes, A. (2009) *The impact of adult support staff on pupils and mainstream schools*. EPPI-Centre Report No. 17021T. EPPI-Centre, Institute of Education.

Alexander, R. (2017) Developing Dialogue: Process, Trial, Outcomes, 17th, *Biennial EARLI Conference*, Tampere, Finland Symposium H4, 31 August 2017, Professional Development in Dialogic Teaching: commonalities and constraints.

Ainsworth, M. (1973) The development of mother-infant attachment. In B. M. Caldwell and H.N. Ricciutti (eds), *Review of Child Development research*, vol. 3. Chicago: University of Chicago Press.

Anda, F. A., Butchart, A., Felitti, V. J. and Brown, D. W. (2010) Building a Framework for Global Surveillance of the Public Health Implications of Adverse Childhood Experiences. *Am J Prev Med*, 2010; 39: 93–98.

Anderson, L. W. and Krathwohl, D. R., (Eds.) (2001) *A Taxonomy for Learning, Teaching, and Assessing: A Revision of Bloom's Taxonomy of Educational Objectives*, Boston, MA: Allyn & Bacon.

Baskind, S. and Thompson, D. (1995) Using assistants to support the educational needs of pupils with learning difficulties: The sublime or the ridiculous? *Educational and Child Psychology*, 12(2), 46–57.

Behaviour is a national problem in schools in England, a recent review finds, The Guardian, March 24, 2017 (online) available from: https://www.theguardian.com/education/2017/mar/24/behaviour-is-a-national-problem-in-schools-in-england-review-finds (accessed 26 October 2017).

Bennett, T. (2017) *Creating a Culture: How school leaders can optimise behaviour*, DfE: London.

Bentham, S. and Hutchins, R. (2012) *Improving Pupil Motivation Together: Teachers and teaching assistants working collaboratively*, Oxon: Routledge.

Bentham, S. (2011) *An Exploration of Collaborative Relationships between Teachers and Teaching Assistants*, unpublished Institution-Focused Study, Institute of Education, University of London.

Bentham, S. (2011) *A Teaching Assistant's Guide to Child Development and Psychology in the Classroom*. 2nd edition, London: Routledge.

Bentham, S. (2016) Improving Pupil Motivation Together, unpublished thesis, Institute of Education, University of London.

Berger, R. (2012) *An Ethic of Excellence: Building a Culture of Craftsmanship with Students*, Portsmouth, NH: Heinemann.

Blatchford, P., Russell, A. and Webster, R. (2012) *Reassessing the Impact of TAs: How Research Challenges Practice and Policy*. Oxon: Routledge.

Blatchford, P., Webster, R. and Russell, A. (2013) *Challenging the Role and Deployment of TAs in Mainstream Schools: The Impact on schools*. Final Report on the Effective Deployment of TAs (EDTA) Project. London: Department of Psychology and Human Development, Institute of Education, University of London.

Bloom, B .S. and Krathwohl, D. R. (1956) *Taxonomy of Educational Objectives: The Classification of Educational Goals*, by a committee of college and university examiners. Handbook: Cognitive Domain. New York: Longmans, Green.

Bomber, L. M. (2011) *What About Me? Inclusive Strategies to Support Pupils with Attachment Difficulties Make it Through the School Day*, Duffield: Worth Publishing Ltd.

Bomber, L. M. (2013) *Settling Troubled Pupils to Learn: Why Relationships Matter in School*, Duffield: Worth Publishing Ltd.

Bomber, L. M. (2007) *Inside I'm Hurting: Practical Strategies for Supporting Children with Attachment Difficulties in Schools*. Duffield: Worth Publishing Ltd.

Booth, T. and Ainscow, M. (2016) *Index for Inclusion: A Guide to School Development Led by Inclusive Values*, 4th edition, Bristol: Centre for Studies on Inclusive Education (CSIE).

Bosanquet, P., Radford, J. and Webster, R. (2016) *The Teaching Assistant's Guide to Effective Interaction: How to Maximise Your Practice*, Oxon: Routledge.

Brophy, J. and Good, T. (1970) *Teacher-student Relationships: Causes and Consequences*. New York: Holt, Rinehart & Winston.

Brown, G. and Wragg, E. C. (1993) *Questioning*, London: Routledge.

Buckley, S. (2002) The significance of early reading for children with Down syndrome, in *Down Syndrome News and Update*, 2(1) April 2002 (online) available from: https://assets.cdn.down-syndrome.org/pubs/a/dsnu-2-1.pdf?_ga=2.162727420.1189014294.1520425298-928394807.1520425298 (accessed 7 March 2018).

Byron, T. (2009) 'We see children as pestilent', *The Guardian*, 17 March 2009. (online) available from: https://www.theguardian.com/education/2009/mar/17/ephebiphobia-young-people-mosquito (accessed 26 October 2017).

Children Act (1989) (online) available from: http://www.legislation.gov.uk/ukpga/1989/41/contents/enacted, (accessed 3 January 2018).

Children and Families Act (2014) (online) available from: http://www.legislation.gov.uk/ukpga/2014/6/pdfs/ukpga_20140006_en.pdf (accessed 16 March, 2018).

Clark, S. (2014) *Outstanding Formative Assessment: Culture and Practice*, Abingdon: Hodder Education.

Clarke, E. and Visser, J. (2017) How do teaching assistants view their role in managing behaviour and cultivate their learning and understanding in relation to managing behaviour? *Teacher Education Advancement Network Journal* (TEAN), 9(1), pp. 66–79.

Clayton, T. (1993) From domestic helper to 'assistant teacher' – the changing role of the British classroom assistant. *European Journal of Special Needs Education*, 8 (1), pp. 32–44.

Covey, S. R. (2004) *The 7 Habits of Highly Effective People*, New York: Simon and Schuster.

Covey, S. R. (2018) Books: *The 7 Habits of Highly Effective People – Habit 2: Begin With The End In Mind*, (online) available from: https://www.stephencovey.com/7habits/7habits-habit2.php (accessed on 20 March 2018).

Deci, E. and Ryan, R. M. (2008). Self-determination theory: A macrotheory of human motivation, development and health. *Canadian Psychology*, 49(3), 182–185.

Deci, E. L. and Moller, A. C. (2005) The concept of competence: A starting place for understanding intrinsic motivation and self-determined extrinsic motivation. In Elliot, A. J. and Dweck, C. S. (eds.) *Handbook of Competence and Motivation*. pp. 579–597. New York: Guilford Press.

Deci, E. L. (2012) *Promoting Motivation, Health, and Excellence* (online) available from: https://www.youtube.com/watch?v=VGrcets0E6I (accessed 26 October 2017).

Department for Education (DfE) (1994) *Code of Practice on the Identification and Assessment of Special Educational Needs*, London: HMSO.

Department for Education (DfE) (2017) *School Workforce in England: November 2016*, SFR25/2017, 22 June 2017.

Department for Education and Department of Health (2015) *Special educational needs and disability code of practice: 0 to 25 years* (online) available at: https://www.gov.uk/government/publications/send-code-of-practice-0-to-25 (accessed 14 August 2017).

Department for Education and Employment (DfEE) (2001) *Special Educational Needs Code of Practice*. London: HMSO.

Department for Education and Skills (DfES) (2003) *Raising Standards and Tackling Workload: a national agreement*. London: DfES Publications.

Department for Education and Skills (DfES) (2004) *Every Child Matters: Change for Children*. Nottingham: DfES Publications.

Department of Education and Science (DES) (1967) *Children and their Primary Schools. A report of the Central Advisory Council for Education* (England) Vol 1. (Plowden Report) London: HMSO.

Department of Education and Science (DES) (1978) *Special Educational Needs: Report of the committee of Enquiry into the Education of Handicapped Children and Young People* (The Warnock Report). London: HMSO.

Department for Education (DfE) (2015) *The Prevent Duty: Departmental Advice for Schools and Childcare Providers*, reference: DFE-00174-2015.

Department for Education (DfE) (2013) *Young Person's Guide to Working Together to Safeguard Children*, (online) available from: https://www.

childrenscommissioner.gov.uk/wp-content/uploads/2017/07/Working-together-to-safeguard-children.pdf (accessed 23 March 2018).

Department for Education (DfE) (2014) *Promoting Fundamental British Values as Part of SMSC in Schools: Departmental Advice for MaintainedSschools*, (online) available from: https://www.gov.uk/government/uploads/system/uploads/attachment_data/file/380595/SMSC_Guidance_Maintained_Schools.pdf (accessed 23 March 2018).

Department for Education (DfE) (2016) *Keeping Children Safe in Education: Statutory Guidance for Schools and Colleges*, (online) available from: https://www.gov.uk/government/uploads/system/uploads/attachment_data/file/550511/Keeping_children_safe_in_education.pdf (accessed 23 March 2018).

Department for Education (DfE) (2017) *School Workforce in England*: November 2016, SFR 25/2017, 22 June 2017.

Department for Education (DfE) (2014) *Supporting Pupils with Medical Conditions atSschool: Statutory Guidance for Governing Bodies of Maintained Schools and Proprietors of Academies in England*, (online) available from: https://www.gov.uk/government/uploads/system/uploads/attachment_data/file/638267/supporting-pupils-at-school-with-medical-conditions.pdf (accessed 23 March 2018).

DoH NHS England (2015) *Future in Mind: Children and Young People's Mental Wellbeing* (online) available from: https://www.gov.uk/government/uploads/system/uploads/attachment_data/file/414024/Childrens_Mental_Health.pdf (accessed 16 October 2017).

Dunne, L., Goddard, G. and Woolhouse, C. (2008) Starting a Foundation degree: teaching assistants self-perceptions of their personal and professional identities, Paper presented at the 38th *Annual SCUTREA Conference*, 2–4 July 2008 University of Edinburgh.

Dweck, C. (2015) Growth Mindset, Revisited, *Education Week*, 35(5) 20, 24.

Dweck, C. (2017) *Mindset-Updated Edition: Changing The Way You think to Fulfil your Potential*, London: Robinson.

Eagleman, D. (2015) *The Brain: The Story of You*. Great Britain: Canongate Books Ltd.

Eraut, M. (1994) *Developing Professional Knowledge and Competence*. London: Falmer Press.

Education Act (1993) (online) available from: http://www.legislation.gov.uk/ukpga/1993/35/contents (accessed 3 January 2018).

Education Act (1981) (online) available from: http://www.legislation.gov.uk/ukpga/1981/60/enacted (accessed 3 March 2018).

Education Act (1996) (online) available from: http://www.legislation.gov.uk/ukpga/1996/56/contents, (accessed 3 January 2018).

Education Reform Act (1988) (online) available from: http://www.legislation.gov.uk/ukpga/1988/40/contents, (accessed 26 March 2018).

Emerson, E. and Hatton, C. (2007) *The Mental Health of Children and Adolescents with Learning Disabilities in Britain*, Institute of Health Research, Lancaster University.

Equality Act (2010) London: The Stationary Office.

Equality and Human Rights Commission (EHRC) (2014) Public Sector Equality Duty Guidance for Schools in England.

Farrer, F. (2010). Re-visiting the 'Quiet Revolution'. In T. Lovat, R. Toomey and N. Clement (Eds.), *International Research Handbook on Values Education and Student Wellbeing*, pp. 395–408, Dordrecht, Netherlands: Spring.

Feinstein, L. and Duckworth, K. (2006) *Development in the early years: Its importance for school performance and adult outcome*, Centre for Research on the Wider Benefits of Learning, Institute of Education, London.

Fredricks, J. A. (2014) *Eight Myths of Student Disengagement: Creating Classrooms of Deep Learning*, London: Sage.

Gardner, H. (1983) *Frames of Mind: The Theory of Multiple Intelligences*, New York: Basic Books.

Gathercole, S. and Alloway, T. (2008). *Working Memory and Learning: APpractical Guide*. London: Sage.

Geddes, H. (2005) *Attachment in the Classroom: The Links Between Children's Early Experience, Emotional Well-being and Performance in School*, London: Worth Publishers.

Gerhardt, S. (2004) *Why Love Matters: How Affection Shapes a Baby's Brain*. Hove: Routledge.

Gibbs, G. (1988). *Learning by Doing: A Guide to Teaching and Learning Methods*. Oxford: Oxford Further Education Unit.

Gilman, S. (2001) Make in up as you go along, *The Evening Standard*, Wednesday, 12 December 2001, p. 28.

Gladwell, M. (2008). *Outliers: The Story of Success*, New York: Little, Brown and Co.

Goldacre, B. (2008). *Bad Science*. Great Britain: Fourth Estate.

Goldin-Meadow S., Levine, S. C., Hedges L. V., Huttenlocher, J., Raudenbush, S. W., and Small S. L. (2014). New evidence about language and cognitive development based on a longitudinal study. *Am. Psychol.* 69:588–99.

Goleman, D. (1996) *Emotional Intelligence: Why It Can Matter More Than IQ*, London: Bloomsbury Publishing.

Goleman, D. (2004) *Emotional Intelligence and Working with Emotional Intelligence*, London: Bloomsbury.

Goswami, U. (2015) *Children's Cognitive Development and Learning*. York: Cambridge Primary Review Trust.

Green, R. W. (2009) *Lost at School*, London: Scribner.

Grierson, J. (2017) Hundreds of knives seized in 18 months at UK schools, figures show, *The Guardian, 12 May 2017. (online) available from:* https://www.theguardian.com/uk-news/2017/may/12/hundreds-of-knives-seized-in-18-months-at-uk-schools-figures-reveal-show-police-england-wales-weapons (accessed 26 October 2017).

Gross, J. (2013) *Time to Talk: implementing outstanding practice in speech, language and communication*, London: Routledge.

Hammer, C. (2012) 'Parent child communication is important from birth.' *Perspective*, March 2012; 15–20.

Hampshire County Council (2017) Make it worthwhile, (online) available from: http://www3.hants.gov.uk/emotional-wellbeing-mental-health-strategy.pdf (accessed 27 March 2018)

Hargreaves, D. (2011) *Leading a self-improving school system*. Nottingham: National College for School Leadership of schools and children's Services.

Hart B, and Risley, T. R. 1995. *Meaningful Differences in the Everyday Experience of Young American Children*. Baltimore: Paul H. Brookes.

Hart B. and Risley T. (2003) The early catastrophe: the 30 million word gap by age 3 American Educator 27(1):4–9.

Hastings, S. (2003) *Questioning*, (online) available from: https://www.tes.com/news/tes-archive/tes-publication/questioning (accessed 19 March 2018).

Hawkins, K. (2017) *Mindful Teacher Mindful School*, London: Sage.

Hegarty, S. (1985) Integration and Teaching: some lessons for practice. *Educational Research*, 27(1) 9–18.

Helliwell, J., Layard, R. and Sachs, J (2017) *World Happiness F*, (online) available from: http://worldhappiness.report/wp-content/uploads/sites/2/2017/03/HR 17.pdf (accessed 16 October 2017).

Higgins, S., Katsipataki, M., Kokotsaki, D., Coleman, R., Major, L.E., and Coe, R. (2014). The Sutton Trust-Education Endowment Foundation Teaching and Learning Toolkit. London: Education Endowment Foundation

Higgins, S., Katsipataki, M., Villanueva-Aguilera, A. B., Coleman, R., Henderson, P., Major, L. E., Coe, R. and Mason, D. (2016) *The Sutton Trust-Education Endowment Foundation Teaching and Learning Toolkit*. Manual. London: Education Endowment Foundation.

HM Government (2015) *Working together to safeguard children: A guide to inter-agency working to safeguard and promote the welfare of children*, Reference DFE-00130-2015.

Hodgson, A., Clunies-Ross, L. and Hegarty, S. (1984) *Learning Together: Teaching Pupils with Special Educational Needs in the Ordinary School*, Windsor: NfER-Nelson.

House of Commons Library (2017) House of Commons Library briefing on children and young people's mental health policy (online) available from: Researchbriefings.parliament.uk/ResearchBriefing/Summary/CBP-7196, (accessed 26 October 2017).

Houssart, J. (2012) Teaching Assistants and intervention programmes in primary mathematics, in, Smith, C. (Ed) *Proceedings of the British Society for Research in Learning Mathematics*, 32(2): 40–45.

Howard-Jones, P. (2015) 'Rewards' [online] available from: https://youtu.be/n6sHPNM_tBg (accessed 7 October 2017).

Howard-Jones, P. (Ed.) (2012) *Education and Neuroscience. Evidence, Theory and Practical Application*, Abingdon: Routledge.

Howes, A. (2003) Teaching reforms and the impact of paid adult support on participation and learning in mainstream schools. *Support for Learning*. 18(4): 147–153.

Ileris, K. (2007) *How We Learn: Learning and Non-Learning in School and Beyond*. Abingdon: Routledge.

Jarvis, M. (2005) The psychology of effective teaching and learning, Oxford: Open University Press.

Kaufmann, L. (2012) Dyscalculia: Neuroscience and Education, in Howard-Jones, P. (Ed.), (2012) *Education and Neuroscience. Evidence, Theory and Practical Application.* Ch 4 Abingdon: Routledge.

Kisler, J. and McConachie, H. (2010) 'Parental reaction to disability', *Paediatrics and Child Health*, 20(7): 309–314, (online) available from: http://dx.doi.org/10.1016/j.paed.2010.02.010 (accessed 26 October 2017).

Knapp, M., Ardino, V., Brimblecombe, N., Evans-Lacko, S., Iemmi, V., King, D., Snell, T., Murguia, S., Mbeah-Bankas, H., Crane, S., Harris, A., Fowler, D., Hodgekins, J. and Wilson, J. (2016) *Youth Mental Health: New Economic Evidence*, London School of Economics and Political Science, Personal Social Services Research Unit.

Lewis, K., Chamberlain, T., Riggall, A., Gagg, K. and Rudd, P. (2007) *How is the Every Child Matters Agenda Affecting Schools?* Annual Survey of Trends in Education 2007: Schools' Concerns and their Implications for Local Authorities: LGA Research Report 4/07, Slough: NFER

Local Government National Training Organisation (2001) *National Occupational Standards for Teaching/Classroom Assistants*, London: LGNTO.

Logsdon, A. (2018) Common Parent Reactions to a Child's Learning Disability, (online) available from: https://www.verywellfamily.com/parent-reactions-childs-disability-2162643 (accessed 14 March, 2018).

Lorenz, S. (1992) Supporting special needs assistants in mainstream schools, *Educational and Child Psychology*, 9(4): 25–33.

Lorenz, S. (1998) *Effective In-class Support: The Management of Support Staff in Mainstream and Special Schools.* London: David Fulton Publishers.

Masdeu Navarro, F. (2015), 'Learning support staff: A literature review,' *OECD Education Working Papers*, No. 125, Paris: OECD Publishing.

Maslow, A. H. (1943). A theory of human motivation, *Psychological Review*, 50 (4), 370.

Maslow, A. H., Frager, R. and Cox, R. (1970) *Motivation and personality* (Vol. 2, pp. 1887–1904). J. Fadiman, and C. McReynolds (Eds.). New York: Harper & Row.

Miller G. E. (1990) The assessment of clinical skills/competence/performance, *Acad Med* (1990); 65: 63–67.

Moyles, J. and Sushitsky, W. (1997) *Jill of All Trades? Classroom Assistants at KS1 Classes.* London: ATL.

Music, G. (2017) Nurturing natures: Attachment and Children's Emotional, Sociocultural and Brain Development 2nd Edition. Abingdon: Routledge.

Nasen (2014) *SEN Support and the Graduated Approach*, Tamworth, Staffordshire: Nasen.

Nasen (2017) Health visitors report increase in children's communication difficulties, (online) available from: http://www.nasen.org.uk/newsviews/News/News.bercow-10-years-on-report.html (accessed 26 October 2017).

National Autistic Society (2010) *You Need to Know: mental health in children and young people with autism: a guide for parents and carers*, London: The National Autistic Society.

National Institute for Health and Care Excellence (NICE, 2012) *Social and emotional wellbeing: early years*: Public health guideline (online) available from: https://www.nice.org.uk/guidance/ph40/resources/social-and-emotional-wellbeing-early-years-pdf-1996351221445 (accessed 23 March 2018).

National Society for the Prevention of Cruelty to Children (NSPCC) (2018) *Sexting: How to talk to children about the risks of sexting - and what you can do to protect them*, (online) available from: https://www.nspcc.org.uk/preventing-abuse/keeping-children-safe/sexting/ (assessed 16 March 2018).

Nystrand, M., Gamoran, A., Kachur, R. and Prendergast, C. (1997) *Opening dialogue. Understanding the dynamics of language and learning in the English classroom*, London: Teachers College Press.

Office for Standards in Education (Ofsted) (2002) *Teaching Assistants in Primary Schools: an Evaluation of the Quality and Impact of their Work* (HMI Report 434)

Ofsted inspectors pelted with food and jostled in corridors on nightmare school visit, *The Telegraph, May, 2017*. (online) available from: http://www.telegraph.co.uk/news/2017/05/12/ofsted-inspectors-pelted-food-jostled-corridors-nightmare-school/ (accessed 26 October 2017).

Pearson S. E., Chambers, G. N. and Hall, K. W. (2003) Video material as a support to developing effective collaboration between teachers and TAs, *Support for Learning*. 18(2): 83–87.

Petch, J. (2017) How Can Joint Practice Development be Embedded Within My Own School (a Primary Special School), unpublished MA(Ed) dissertation, Institute of Education, University of Chichester.

Piaget, J. (1970) *The Science of Education and the Psychology of the child*, New York: Viking Press.

PriceWaterhouseCoopers (2001) *Teacher Workload Study: final report*. 5 December 2001. PriceWaterhouseCoopers.

Pritchard, A. (2014) *Ways of learning. Learning theories and learning styles in the classroom*. 3rd edition Abingdon: Routledge.

Rae, T, (2016) *Building Positive thinking Habits: Increasing Self-Confidence & Resilience in Young People through CBT*, Buckingham: Hinton House Publishers Ltd.

Richardson, R. and Bolloten, B. (2015) 'Fundamental British Values' Origins, controversy, ways forward: a symposium. *Race Equality Teaching*, (online) available from: http://www.insted.co.uk/british-values.pdf (accessed 23 March 2018).

Ringrose, J., Gill, R., Livingstone, S. and Harvey, L. (2012) A Qualitative Study of Children, Young People and 'Sexting', NSPCC: London.

Rosenthal, R. and Jacobson, L. (1966) Teachers' expectancies: determinants of pupils' IQ gains, *Psychological Reports*. 19: 115–18.

Royal College of Nursing. (2017) *Child and Adolescent Mental Health Key Facts* [Online] available from: https://www.evidence.nhs.uk/Search?om=[{%22srn%22:[%22Royal%20College%20of%20Nursing%20-%20RCN%22]}]&q=recent+statistics+on+self+harm+and+suicide&sp=on (accessed 16 October 2017).

Ryan, R. M. and Deci, E. L. (2000) Intrinsic and extrinsic motivations: Classic definitions and new directions, *Contemporary Educational Psychology*, 25: 54–67.

Ryan, R. M., and Deci, E. L. (2002) An overview of self-determination theory. In E. L. Deci and R. M. Ryan (Eds.), *Handbook of self-determination research* (pp. 3–33). Rochester, NY: University of Rochester Press.

Schön, D. A. (1983) The Reflective Practitioner: How Professionals Think in Action. London: Temple Smith

Sharples, J., Webster, R. and Blatchford, P. (2015) *Making Best Use of Teaching Assistant Guidance Report*, Education Endowment Fund, (online) available from: https://v1.educationendowmentfoundation.org.uk/uploads/pdf/TA_Guidance_Report_Interactive.pdf, (accessed 23 March 2018).

Sinek, S. (2009) Start With Why: How Great Leaders Inspire Everyone to Take Action, London: Penguin.

Statistics UK (2013a) *School Workforce in England: November 2013*, National Statistics, Department for Education, United Kingdom.

Statistics UK (2013b) *Schools, Pupils and Their Characteristics: January 2014*, National Statistics, Department for Education, United Kingdom.

Stonewall (2017) *School Report: The Experiences of Lesbian, Gay, Bi and Trans Young People in Britain's Schools in 2017*, (online) available from: http://www.stonewall.org.uk/school-report-2017 (accessed 16 March 2018).

Swaab, D. (2014) *We Are Our Brains: From the Womb to Alzheimer's*, London: Penquin.

The Education Reform Act (1988) London: HMSO (online) available from: http://www.legislation.gov.uk/ukpga/1988/40/contents (accessed 3 January 2018).

Times Education Supplement (TES) Teaching assistant pay and conditions (2017) (online) available from: https://www.tes.com/jobs/careers-advice/teaching-assistant/teaching-assistant-pay-and-conditions (accessed 26 March 2018).

The Guardian, Secret Teaching Assistant: We end up hindering the pupils we're meant to help, November 12th (online) available from: https://www.theguardian.com/teacher-network/2016/nov/12/secret-teaching-assistant-we-end-up-hindering-the-pupils-were-meant-to-help (accessed 26 March 2018).

Training Development Agency for Schools (TDA) (2007) *National Occupational Standards in Supporting Teaching and Learning in Schools*, London: TDA.

Tripp, D. (1993). *Critical Incidents in Teaching: Developing Professional Judgement*. London: Routledge.

UK Council for Child Internet Safety (UKCCIS) (2017) *Sexting in schools and colleges: Responding to incidents and safeguarding young people*, (online) available from: https://www.gov.uk/government/uploads/system/uploads/attachment_data/file/609874/6_2939_SP_NCA_Sexting_In_Schools_FINAL_Update_Jan17.pdf, (accessed 16 March 2018).

Unison (2016) School support staff facing high levels of violence and abuse, (online) available online at: https://www.unison.org.uk/news/press-release/

2016/06/school-support-staff-facing-high-levels-of-violence-and-abuse-says-unison/ (accessed 26 October 2017).

Unison Survey (2016) Bad Form: Behaviour in Schools, (online) available from: https://www.unison.org.uk/content/uploads/2016/06/Behaviour-in-Schools.pdf (accessed 26 October 2017).

Vygotsky, L. S. (1986) *Thought and Language*, (Ed) A. Kozulin, Cambridge, MA: MIT Press.

Workforce Agreement Monitoring Group (WAMG) (2008) Raising Standards and Tackling Workload Implementing the national Agreement, Note 22 July 2008.

Webster, R. (2017) The five steps teaching assistants must follow to increase student independence, TES, 26 March, 2017, (online) available from: https://www.tes.com/news/school-news/breaking-views/five-steps-teaching-assistants-must-follow-increase-student, (accessed: 27 February 2018).

Webster, R., Russell, A. and Blatchford, P. (2016) *Maximising the Impact of Teaching Assistants: Guidance for School Leaders and Teachers*, 2nd Edition, Oxon: Routledge.

Weinstein, R. S. (2004) *Reaching Higher: The Power of Expectations in Schooling*. London: Harvard University Press.

West Sussex County Council (2016) Think Family and Early Help, (online) available from: https://www.westsussex.gov.uk/social-care-and-health/social-care-and-health-information-for-professionals/children/think-family/ (accessed 26 October 2017).

West Sussex County Council SEND Local Offer (2018) (online) available from: https://www.westsussex.gov.uk/education-children-and-families/special-educational-needs-and-disability-send/send-local-offer/ (accessed, 14 March, 2018).

Wigley, V., Lindsay, G., and Clough, P. (1989) *The role of special needs support assistants in mainstream school*, Unpublished paper, Special Educational Needs Evaluation and Research Group. Educational Research Centre: Sheffield University.

Willingham, D. T. (2009) *Why Don't Students Like School?* San Francisco, CA: Jossey Bass.

Wilson, E. and Bedford, D. (2008) 'New Partnerships for Learning': teachers and TAs working together in schools - the way forward. *Journal of Education for Teaching*. 34(2): 37–150.

Wilson, V., Schlapp, U. and Davidson, J. (2003) An extra pair of hands? Managing classroom assistants in Scottish primary schools. *Educational Management and Administration*. 31. pp.189–205.

Wilson, R., Sharp, C., Shuayb, M. Kendall, L., Wade, P., and Easton, C. (2007) Research into the deployment and impact of support staff who have achieved HLTA status, London: National Foundation for Educational Research.

Woolfolk, A., Hughes, M. and Walkup, V. (2007) *Psychology in Education*, Harrow: Pearson Education.

Glossary

Active listening is a special type of listening where we communicate to the person with whom we are talking that we have indeed heard and understood what they have said.

Attachment is the bond formed by a baby with the (principal caregiver), the quality of which is said to influence the individual's behaviour and relationships.

Autism spectrum condition (ASC) This refers to a range of difficulties that include social interaction, sensory issues, repetitive behaviours, verbal and nonverbal communication and restricted or fixated interests, which can affect an individual from a mild to severe degree.

Behaviourism is the theory that behaviour can be explained in terms of conditioning, taking no account of thoughts or feelings and that behaviour can be altered through positive rewards or negative consequences.

Cognitive behaviour therapy (CBT) is a therapy that helps individuals understand how their thoughts and feelings influence their behaviours.

Cognitive development is the development of intellectual processes to include thinking, knowing, reasoning, understanding and problem solving.

Cognitive disequilibrium is an unpleasant mental state that results when an individual realises that they cannot fit new experiences into existing schemas. In everyday language, an individual becomes confused when they realise that they don't understand and this motivates them to learn.

Cognitive restructuring is a technique drawn from cognitive behavioural therapy that can help people identify, challenge and alter maladaptive stress-inducing thought patterns and beliefs.

Constructive feedback is a type of feedback that both acknowledges what has been done and what still needs to be done in a manner that is seen as helpful and positive by the individual receiving the feedback.

Constructivism is a learning theory where people are seen as constructing their own understanding and knowledge of the world through experience.

Differentiation is the modification of the curriculum so that all pupils are able to access it. It may be achieved by adapting what is taught or how pupils are required to demonstrate their learning.

Discovery learning is an approach that sees an individual's act of participating in a learning activity as being responsible for the development of new knowledge.

Down syndrome is a chromosomal anomaly where there are forty-seven chromosomes in each cell instead of forty-six. An extra chromosome 21 is responsible for this condition.

Education, Health and Care Plan (EHCP) EHCPs have replaced Statement of Educational Needs since 2015. They are given as a result of a multi-agency statutory assessment and outline the support a pupil with SEND needs to achieve stated outcomes. Pupils and parents should be involved in their production.

Emotional intelligence is demonstrated by emotional self-awareness and the ability to self-regulate emotions and behave empathetically to others.

Ethos in a school is defined as the characteristic spirit of a school as reflected in its aims and values.

Higher level teaching assistant (HLTA) A status given to TAs who reach certain standards of education and performance that enables them to be given greater spheres of responsibility.

INSET In Service Training Day

Intelligence tests are administered by an educational or clinical psychologist to measure cognitive or intellectual ability.

Intrinsic means stemming from within the person.

Meta-cognition is thinking about thinking, for example knowing which strategy to use or knowledge of one's learning strengths and weaknesses.

Metamemory is knowledge about memory, in particular one's own memory abilities.

Multi-sensory techniques are often used in the teaching of phonics. This technique aims to teach through an approach that uses all senses: auditory, visual and kinaesthetic.

Neuroscience   The study of the brain and the nervous system.

NQT   refers to a newly qualified teacher.

NVQ   is a work-based qualification which recognises the skills, knowledge and competencies a person needs to have in a job.

Occupational therapists (OT)   are involved in the assessment and treatment of movement disorders. Occupational therapists assess what daily living skills an individual has and can provide suitable equipment and adaptations to the individual's environment so that they can be as independent as possible.

Pupil premium funding   is additional funding for publicly funded schools in England which aims to raise the attainment of disadvantaged pupils of all abilities and to close the gaps between them and their peers.

Radicalisation   is a process by which a person is influenced to adopt increasingly extreme views that undermine the accepted ideas and expressions of the country where they live.

Resilience factors   are those situations, events, relationships and personality traits that serve to protect an individual from negative conditions such as mental health problems.

Scaffolding   describes the process of help by which a more skilled individual supports a less skilled individual.

Schemas   are organized patterns or units of action or thought that we construct to make sense of our interaction with the world.

Self-actualisation   occurs when an individual has achieved their full potential.

Self-concept   is defined as the whole person. Self-concept can be divided into the self-image, the ideal self and self-esteem.

Self-esteem   is the extent to which one values oneself.

Self-fulfilling prophecy   is the tendency for things to turn out as expected. For example, a teacher who expects a pupil to fail might treat the pupil in a manner that increases the likelihood that they will fail. In this example the teacher's expectations have come true, but the pupil's failure is in part due to the teacher's behaviour.

Self-image   is how an individual describes themselves.

Self-regulation   is the ability to monitor and control our own behaviour, emotions or thoughts.

SEN Code of Practice (2001)   The code of practice outlined a graduated approach to meeting the needs of pupils with SEN to include Early Years Action/School Action and Early Years Action Plus/ School Action Plus, and then to a Statement of SEN if appropriate.

SEND Code of Practice 0-25 years (DfE, DoH, 2015)   This updates the *2001 Code of Practice* introducing one level of SEND support in school and Education Health Care Plans (EHCPs). It emphasises the role of parents and working multi-agencies.

Social learning theory   states that we learn by observing and imitating others.

Special Educational Needs Co-ordinator (SENCo):   The person or persons in school responsible for overseeing the day-to-day operation of special needs provision.

Spiral curriculum   is a concept used by Bruner that sees concepts being developed and redeveloped with increasing levels of complexity as the child progresses through the education system.

Statements of Special Educational Need: Documents regulated by law setting out the educational and non-educational needs of individuals and the provision to be put in place to meet those needs.

Statutory assessment   is a detailed multi-professional assessment to find out exactly what a child's special educational needs are, and is led by the local authority.

Teaching assistant (TA)   A term used within the English school system to refer to individuals who are actively engaged in supporting teaching and learning.

Values   are agreed principles of behaviour and reflect what groups or individuals believe to be important or right.

Working memory   is a psychological model to explain the process of holding information in mind whilst simultaneously processing it.

Index